IT TAKES A CHURCH

EVERY MEMBER'S GUIDE
TO KEEPING YOUNG PEOPLE
SAFE AND SAVED

GARY L. HOPKINS,
M.D., DR. P.H.

AND JOYCE W. HOPP,
PH.D., M.P.H.

Pacific Press® Publishing Association
Nampa, Idaho
Oshawa, Ontario, Canada
www.pacificpress.com

2310

Edited by Jerry D. Thomas
Cover Design by Michelle C. Petz
Inside Design by Steve Lanto

Additional copies of this book may be purchased at
http://www.adventistbookcenter.com

Library of Congress Cataloging-in-Publication Data:

ISBN 0- 8163-1904-9

02 03 04 05 • 5 4 3 2 1

Contents

Matt and His World

Matt is a good kid. He is from a fairly typical family of today. His divorced mother works full time at the post office to support Matt and his younger sister. At his last birthday, Matt turned 15, and he's looking forward to getting his driver's license. He is in his second year of high school.

A typical day in Matt's life might look something like this. He gets up around seven o'clock, eats breakfast, dresses, and is dropped off at school by his mom. When school gets out around three, he catches a ride home with one of his friends who has a car. His little sister usually goes to their grandmother's home, where she spends her after-school hours. Because Matt is not an exceptional athlete, he does not play on any of his high school's teams. His after-school hours are generally filled with activities he picks for himself.

When he arrives home, Matt may play video games for a while, watch television, or pull out a video from his collection. Or he may call a friend to come and pick him up so they can ride around town looking for something to do—or just looking for girls.

Because Matt generally respects his mother's rules, he usually arrives home around six for family dinner. His evening hours are typically filled with an hour or so of studying, then an hour or two of surfing the Internet on the computer his grandfather gave him for Christmas. Or, he may watch television or play more video games.

One thing that Matt looks forward to each week is Wednesday evening when he goes with a couple of friends to visit several elderly people at a local nursing home. He doesn't spend a lot of time doing this, maybe an hour or so, but he really looks forward to it.

Matt is a mainstream high-school sophomore who does more good than bad by a long shot. Because his grades in school are reasonably good (B's and C's), and he generally stays out of trouble both at home and school, his mother doesn't feel that she needs to pressure him to study more. She doesn't spend time lecturing him on the need to avoid things like alcohol, tobacco, or drugs. She does take time just about every evening to chat with him—just friendly mother-son conversations.

She often tells him how she is concerned for him and that she often fears that he might someday get involved with drugs or one of the other dangers that seem to surround kids of his age. There are no harsh threats—just caring conversations. Matt knows that his mother cares for him and clearly understands her position regarding the choices that he is already facing day-to-day. His mother feels that one main reason he has generally stayed out of trouble is that the family attends church together every weekend; they never miss.

So Matt is doing fairly well. He really is a good kid. So let's explore what is going on around Matt during his journey through his teen years.

Matt attends a typical high school, one not much different from the one down the street from where you live. At his school, if you asked the students if any of them had carried a gun on one or more days during the past month, almost 6% would say "yes." If you also asked the same students if any of them had carried any weapon (gun, knife, club, etc.) on school property during the past month, 12.5% would say "yes." If you continued to examine the threat of physical harm at Matt's high school, you would learn that in any given month, just over 4% actually skipped school on at least one day because they felt unsafe. During any given month, 7.4% would report that they had been threatened or injured with a weapon on school property one or more times. Almost 15% would tell you that they had been in at least one physical fight on school property during the previous school year. Further, more than 20% seriously considered attempting suicide (15.1% for males and 27.1% for females), and 15.7% (12.2% for males and 20.0% for females) actually made a plan about how they would attempt suicide during the previous school year. All of this at Matt's high school, a fairly typical one.

Does all of this sound pretty rough? Well, it is. But, let's look further.

We are all quite aware that smoking is not good for health. In fact, at Matt's school the students have been taught quite a bit of information over the years about the dangers of tobacco. If you were to give his classmates a quiz and asked them about the ill effects of tobacco, you would find that most would understand that tobacco use is dangerous. But has this information resulted in these same kids avoiding tobacco use? Let's look.

A survey of Matt's classmates would show that more than 70% have tried cigarette smoking in their lives. Remember—these are students who have been taught that cigarette smoking is harmful to health. Of those who had tried a cigarette, just fewer than 25% of them tried their first cigarette before the age of 13 years. If you ask them where they get their cigarettes, you would find that almost 30% purchased the cigarettes themselves in a store or a gas station sometime during the past month. Of those who purchased the cigarettes themselves, only one-third were asked to show proof of age at the time of purchase.

A striking 31.9% of the students who have tried cigarettes would report that they had already tried to quit smoking. Does this concern you? If it doesn't consider this: "Of teenagers who are able to smoke two cigarettes to completion, 85% will become regular smokers" (Sells & Blum, 1996). The typical students at Matt's school who are quite well educated about tobacco use and its related problems are using tobacco at fairly high rates, and a third of them have already tried to quit.

Alcohol use is a common problem in adults, but its roots begin at early ages, even at Matt's school. Of Matt's classmates who have used alcohol, about a third of them took their first drink (more than just a few sips) before the age of 13 years. Of his peers, 80 percent have had at least one drink on one or more days, over half use alcohol at least monthly, and a third of them binge drink (consuming five or more drinks of alcohol in a row) at least monthly.

Do you remember that Matt often rides home from school with friends? Well, sometimes these friends may drink and drive. Of Matt's classmates during any given month, more than 36% rode at least once in a vehicle driven by someone who had been drinking alcohol, and 17% drove a vehicle after drinking alcohol. Alcohol use among the students at Matt's school is a problem. Remember, his school is a typical one, much like the ones in your town.

Marijuana use has become a major problem for young people in recent years. Of Matt's peers, about 10% used marijuana before the age of 13 years, almost half have used it sometime, and just over a quarter of them use it during any given month.

Matt has heard more and more about sex at school. He is aware that even among his friends, having sex is very common. If we surveyed his classmates, we would learn that just less than half were sexually experienced and over seven percent of them had their first sexual experience before the age of 13 years. Of his classmates who were having sex, one in six had experienced sexual intercourse with four or more partners. Fully one quarter of them drank alcohol or used drugs before their most-recent sexual experience.

The rates of sexual activity among young people is disturbing as it has the potential to lead to unexpected pregnancy and the risk of sexually transmitted diseases. Regarding pregnancy, 50% of all teen pregnancies occur within the first six months after the initial intercourse (Zabin & Clark, 1983). In the U.S., more than 1 million women under the age of 20 become pregnant each year. Teen mothers are more likely to drop out of school and are less likely to attend college than other teens. Only 30% of the girls at Matt's school who become pregnant as teens will finish high school. And, the babies of teen mothers also suffer. These youngsters are more likely to have childhood health problems, require more hospitalizations, and perform less well on cognitive tests than peers (Sells et al., 1996).

Fully two-thirds of all cases of sexually transmitted diseases are found in youth under the age of 25 years. In the US, three million teens are diagnosed with a sexually transmitted disease each year. This is not a simple problem. Many of the organisms that cause these infections can lead to very serious health consequences. A virus that causes genital warts, called the human papilloma virus is responsible for responsible for 50% of all cervical cancer cases in women (CDC, 2000). Did you get that? A virus common in our young people transmitted through sex, a behavior common among our young people, accounts for half of all cases of cervical cancer in women—sex to infection to cancer.

If that isn't enough, more than half of all of the new cases of HIV/AIDS in the world are found in individuals less than 25 years of age—our youth (UNAIDS, 1999).

So tobacco, alcohol, drugs, and sex are very commonly found in Matt's typical high school—in Matt's world. But let's look further. Matt spends quite a bit of his time by himself. He watches television and surfs the Internet.

The typical American home—Matt's home and maybe your home—has the television turned on (but not necessarily viewed) for an average of 7 hours and 13 minutes per day (Dietz & Strasburger, 1991). As more people gain access to satellite and cable stations, these numbers will probably increase. By age 70, most people will have watched the television for between 7 and 10 years of their lives (Derksen and Strasburger, 1994).

The average 18 year-old has already watched 22,000 hours of television (21 to 23 hours per week)—more time than he or she has spent in school (12,000 hours by the end of high school)! Young people have been exposed to 350,000 commercials by the time they turn 21 (Dietz et al., 1991).

The Kaiser Family Foundation recently funded an extensive review of the research literature on young people's exposure to media, along with other media-related issues. The results are alarming. The typical American child 2 to 8 years of age spends 5.5 hours per day with various types of electronic media. This number increases to 7.25 hours for children ages 8 to 18 (Roberts & Christensen, 2000). It doesn't require advanced mathematics to figure out that television, movies, radio, CDs, tapes, computers, and print media consume well over a third of the waking hours of young people today.

Cyberspace, a place where Matt spends a considerable amount of his daily time, is not a place for young people to roam without supervision. The U.S. Congress recently heard testimony about a survey of 5,000 regular Web users, aged 10 to 17. Nearly one in five said that they had experienced sexual advances online, and a quarter said they had been sent obscene pictures (*Christian Science Monitor,* 2000).

The Internet is the newest of the media. It combines both wonderful resources and horrible risks. "The Internet is as persistent as it is potent, an indelible and uncontainable presence in the culture. In fact, the Internet isn't separate from the culture at all; it is the culture. All the trash, flotsam and spillage of our society gets its moments there, and the tiniest obsession has its spot on the shelf, right next to Bach and charity and sunsets. The Internet lets a million flowers bloom, and a million weeds" (Javier, Herron, and Primavara, 1998).

The number of pornographic sites available to Matt on the Internet, free of charge, may range into the 100,000s or even more. What good could come of this?

When you see Matt at the store, school or church, you will notice his broad smile and vibrant youth. You can't read his face and determine all that is going on around him on a daily basis or even identify all of the traps that lie in his path. Matt is growing up in a world where an awful lot can go wrong.

If we wait until Matt is around 14 or 15 years of age to address the potential hazards that face him—that is, wait until Matt has experimented with drugs or sex or has been severely influenced by many different media exposures—we are starting much too late. Knowing the potential problems, we need to start much earlier in his life. You say that all of this is his mother's job? True enough, to a point. But kids need more than parents. They need others; they need a community of caring adults.

As we discuss what can be done, let's keep a keen focus on prevention. Let's try to keep bad things from happening in Matt's life. If we don't, we will be looking at trying to decide what to do for him once he has experienced drugs or become infected with the virus that causes AIDS. Once a person has tried something, getting him to quit is a much different issue from working to prevent that same behavior.

But, even if Matt does experiment and get involved in dangerous behaviors, let's not give up. Let's look at what we can do. If this challenge seems impossible, have courage! By banding together, we can make a difference!

Unless otherwise cited, all data from this chapter are from the 1997 Youth Risk Behavior Survey, conducted by the Centers for Disease Control and Prevention. www.cdc.gov/nccdphp/dash

Centers for Disease Control and Prevention. (December 2000). *CDC Issues Major New Report on STD Epidemics: Gonorrhea Rates Increase From 1997 To 1999, Suggesting Possible Reversal of Two-Decade Decline; Syphilis Rates at All Time Low; First-of-its-Kind Research on HPV Also Released.* http://www.cdc.gov/nchstp/dstd/Press_Releases/ STDEpidemics2000.htm

Christian Science Monitor (2000) "Kids and Smut on the Web," 92(145)(June): 8.

Derksen D. J., and V. C. Strasburger. 1994. "Children and the Influence of the Media," *Primary Care* 21(4): 747–758.

Dietz, W. H,. and V. C. Strasburger. 1991. "Children, Adolescents, and Television," *Current Problems in Pediatrics* 21: 8–31.

Javier, R. A., W. G. Herron, and L. Primavera. 1998. "Violence and the Media: A Psychological Analysis," *International Journal of Instructional Media* 25(4): 339–356.

Roberts, D. F. and P. G. Christenson. (February 2000). *Here's Looking at You, Kid: Alcohol, Drugs and Tobacco in the Entertainment in Media.* http://www.kff.org.

Sells, C. W., and Blum, R. W. 1996. "Current Trends in Adolescent Health." In *Handbook of Adolescent Health Risk Behaviors*, Eds. R. J. DiClemente, W. B. Hansen, and L. Ponton, New York: Plenum Press.

UNAIDS (1999). *Facts and Figures: 1999 World AIDS Campaign.* www.unaids.org/wac/1999/eng/facts-e.doc.

Zabin, L. S. and S. D. Clark. 1983. "Institutional Factors Affecting Teenager's Choice and Reasons for Delay in Attending a Family Planning Clinic. *Family Planning Perspectives, 15* no.1: 25–29.

Education/ Information

When Matt was in elementary school, he attended the same kinds of classes your neighbors' kids or your own children might have—mathematics, history, geography, reading, and so on. As he moved through the lower grades, the curriculum contained more and more information related to health. He was taught about good food and bad food, although at lunchtime his school cafeteria menu often conflicted with what he had been taught, serving meals very high in fat. That was a little confusing to Matt but he, like most of us, shrugged his shoulders and forged on through school.

He learned about the heart and the muscles; and in the third or fourth grade, he started learning about the brain, lungs, and digestive tract. He learned how substances such as tobacco, alcohol, and other drugs can cause harm to these organs. In the fifth and sixth grade, his teachers started to teach about human reproduction, the testicles (the kids giggled) and the ovaries (that sounded so much more scientific and serious). They learned about conception and where babies come from. Eventually they leaned about sex. About the same time that the teachers started focusing on sex, they also began teaching quite a bit about drugs, including tobacco and alcohol.

The teachers used several different methods to teach these topics. Matt recalls a very disturbing movie shown in class. It was an actual film of an operation where a surgeon made an incision on the chest of an older man; blood squirted everywhere and the kids groaned. Some of them became a little light-headed and turned pale. Then the movie showed the man's chest cavity being opened, with large chrome instruments used to push back the ribs and hold the chest open. Then they saw the lung. It was black and ugly. The doctor clamped arteries and veins as he removed the entire lung and laid the bloody, black organ on a table. Then the surgeon cut the lung open and displayed a thick, hard mass about the size of a tennis ball.

Matt wasn't sure what that was until the doctor explained that this was a tumor— cancer. He went on to explain that this man had smoked most of his life and that this ugly mass was the result of the use of tobacco. How terrible! Who would ever smoke cigarettes?

Another day, a nurse pushed a little old woman into class in a wheelchair. The woman had green tubes that crossed over each of her ears and met under her nose. Little tubes entered each nostril. A long tube was hooked to a tank that the nurse explained contained oxygen to help the woman breathe. There was a silver gadget sticking out of the woman's neck, right in front. When the she wanted to talk, she had to put her finger over the tube, then gasp for air as a few words came from her mouth. She told the kids not to smoke.

The nurse went on to describe how people who smoke eventually ruin their lungs and develop a condition called emphysema. The teacher wrote the term on the blackboard and told the kids to learn it and know how to spell it correctly as they would see it again on a test in class.

The woman showed her very blue fingers that looked like clubs, also caused by smoking. She unbuttoned the top two buttons on her blouse and showed the top of a railroad-track-looking scar that she explained went down almost to her belly button. The nurse explained that 10 years ago her patient had undergone open-heart surgery. The arteries that supplied the wall of the woman's heart had become almost completely blocked because of her tobacco use, and she needed this very serious operation in order to live without chest pain. Then she pulled down a sock on one of her ankles and showed a long scar that went down the inside of her inner leg. That is where the surgeon had operated to remove a long vein to use to furnish blood to her heart.

The kids were allowed to ask questions of this very brave but severely ill woman. She answered them the best she could although it was difficult for her to speak. The nurse helped out by filling in when the woman couldn't continue. The woman explained that she had smoked for 50 years. One of Matt's classmates asked if after she had smoked for 20 years couldn't she tell that something was going wrong with her health. The answer was, "yes," but she explained that she just couldn't quit smoking. She smoked even after she knew it was hurting her. The teacher wrote the word *addiction* on the board—another word to memorize for that upcoming test.

What a vivid picture! The kids were shocked and vowed never to smoke. They even signed commitments—written contracts—confirming that their lives would be tobacco free.

When Matt was in the sixth grade, a police officer brought a man in handcuffs to class. He was obviously in trouble and wore a red outfit that had "County Jail" stenciled on the back. The man had tattoos everywhere: arms, neck, even his forehead. He also had long dark scars on the insides of both arms. These scars looked terrible. His skin and eyes had turned yellow. He looked awful!

The man told his story. When he was young he started smoking cigarettes and then marijuana. Eventually he tried cocaine and really liked it. He started to steal from hardware stores to get things to sell so that he could have money for drugs. Eventually he began using heroin that he injected into the veins of his arms. That is where those ugly scars came from. Gross!

His drug use caused him to drop out of school. He got married at 17, but his wife left him within the first year, taking his baby son with her. He started stealing from his parents and other family members; all of his close relatives eventually turned their backs on him. He found friends on the street whom he used drugs with. He drank heavily. Eventually he robbed a bank and shot an employee, who survived; for that he was sentenced to 17 years in jail on a number of charges, including attempted murder.

Matt and his classmates were allowed to ask questions. They learned that the man's yellow color came from drinking so much alcohol that his liver was failing. This was called *jaundice*—another word to learn. The man pled with the kids not to start using tobacco, marijuana, or even alcohol. He actually cried as he told his life story.

Who would want to live like that? Matt's classmates decided that day that drugs were not for them.

After all of these exercises, the teachers tested the students on what they had learned. The tests didn't seem difficult. It was pretty much common sense. Tobacco use causes lung disease and also problems with the heart and blood vessels. Alcohol use can cause liver disease, high blood pressure, ulcers, suppression of the immune system, and more. The average score earned by Matt and his classmates was always higher than 95%. They knew their stuff when it came to health—especially about tobacco, alcohol, and drugs.

During the last half of Matt's sixth-grade year, his teacher purchased a very expensive sex-education curriculum. It came with workbooks, professional videos, and all sorts of exercises for the students to do relating to sex, diseases that are transmitted among sexual partners, and HIV/AIDS. They studied about teen pregnancy and its related consequences. They actually had a ceremony where students publicly vowed to remain sexually abstinent until marriage. They recited their vows one at a time. Matt's mom was present and she was tearfully proud. All of Matt's classmates made commitments at the very special event.

In addition to the movie of the man with lung cancer, the woman in the wheelchair, the yellow-skinned inmate, the sex-education class, and the formal abstinence-commitment ceremony, Matt's teachers kept a regular program going. They arranged to show at least weekly videos and to arrange for some guest lecturers who discussed many of the harmful features of living an unhealthful lifestyle, especially in the areas of drugs and sex.

Sometimes the school principal would bring in nationally noted experts to talk about these issues. In church, Matt's pastor would preach on the need to avoid these dangers; he talked about the body being the temple of God and how getting involved in any of these dangerous activities was sin and would have long-term consequences. Matt was pretty much inundated with information. He could almost write a term paper on any of these areas without spending too much time at the library.

When Matt was in his first year of high school however, he noticed that one of his classmates, Candy, wasn't coming to class anymore. He eventually learned that she had gotten pregnant and dropped out of school. How could that be? Candy was an almost straight-A student. She had taken all of the same classes as Matt, she knew about reproductive anatomy and scored very high in her sex-education course, she had taken the abstinence vow, was a member of the same church that Matt attended—yet she got pregnant. Matt had to think about this one. What went wrong?

By the time Matt was in his second year of high school, 70% of his classmates had at least tried tobacco, and about a third of them smoked regularly. By then, 80% had tried alcohol, and a third of them were binge drinkers. About half had tried marijuana and many used it regularly, and half of his class was sexually experienced. So, go figure! Or as kids might say, "What's up with that?"

Matt and his peers knew pretty much all they needed to know about these issues, yet this information somehow didn't translate into their avoidance of these potentially dangerous behaviors.

One night Matt, his little sister, Uncle Vanny, and mom were out enjoying some ice cream. They were sitting at a table and chatting when a woman who must have weighed in excess of 400 pounds came in, ordered a huge banana split, and sat down several tables away to enjoy her treat. Matt's little sister whispered, "Doesn't she know why she is so large and that the banana split isn't good for her?" Mom didn't say much except a soft "shh."

Matt said, "That's sort of like my classmates. They know drugs are dangerous, they have learned about it in school for years, but for some reason they still do it."

Mom shrugged her shoulders; little sister didn't respond. Then Matt's mom said, "Who could possibly understand the consequences of being overweight better than that woman? She must be an expert at it. I don't think she doesn't know. I wonder why living with sore joints, struggling to find clothes that fit, and suffering the stares of rude onlookers hasn't inspired her to lose weight or at least avoid ice cream?" Uncle Vanny didn't say anything; he just listened, as he knew his belly was pretty big too.

Knowledge about the dangers of risky behaviors does not necessarily translate into the avoidance of those behaviors. Sixty-one million Americans smoke and it is doubtful that even one of them isn't aware that smoking is dangerous.

In 1995, we conducted a survey of students attending Seventh-day Adventist high schools throughout North America. The purpose of the study was to measure the level of accurate HIV/AIDS knowledge (can you get AIDS from holding hands? can you get AIDS from a mosquito? etc.) and to measure the behaviors of the students. In total, 1,748 students participated. An analysis of the data revealed that the students who had never had sex had a very high level of AIDS knowledge—their score was 91% correct. But so did the students who had engaged in sex—their score was 89% correct (Hopkins et al., 1998).

A study recently completed at a Caribbean site where several hundred students attend high school revealed that students were generally knowledgeable of modes of transmission of HIV, the virus that causes AIDS; they answered 89% of the questions correctly. But when behaviors were examined, it was found that most of the students were sexually experienced and had engaged in sex with multiple partners (Hopkins et al., 2001).

School-based approaches to smoking prevention have typically been knowledge/information based. In the early 1960s and 1970s, programs were initiated across America to inform students in schools about tobacco. This effort was huge and followed the Surgeon General's report warning that tobacco was dangerous to one's health. The strategy to provide smoking information was based on the assumption that young people who smoke did not understand the health-compromising effects of tobacco (Thompson, 1978). Kids just didn't know enough, so informing them would solve the problem and result in less tobacco use.

One technique that was used along with this information was fear-arousal—attempting to scare kids into not using tobacco. This effort did not work. Kids were no less likely to use tobacco after receiving such educational programs than those who received no information at all. Perry & Staufacker (1996) suggest that adolescents' general knowledge of the adverse health effects of smoking is simply a poor predictor of subsequent use. As behavioral research moves forward, we are learning over and over again that knowledge alone just isn't enough.

All young people need instruction about the obvious harm of drugs and premarital sex, but also about the temptations they will be exposed to on television, videos and the Internet. Education about these problems is not only essential but it should be mandatory. They all need it. But this information alone will not prevent your youngsters from these dangerous behaviors. Education and knowledge is important and essential. But if that is all you do, it probably won't work. So, what does work?

Hopkins, G. L., M. K. Freier, D. McBride, R. J. DiClemente, and T. Babikian. 2001. "HIV/AIDS Knowledge and Risk Behaviors of High School Students in the Caribbean." Unpublished manuscript.

Perry, C. L., and M. J. Staufacker. 1996. "Tobacco Use." *In The Handbook of Adolescent Health Risk Behavior.* Eds. R. J. DiClemente, W. B. Hansen, and L. E. Ponton. Plenum Press: New York.

Thompson, E. L. 1978. "Smoking Education Programs, 1960-1976." *American Journal of Public Health* 68(3): 250–257.

Hopkins, G. L., J. Hopp, H. Hopp Marshak, C. Neish, , and G. Rhoads. 1998. "AIDS Risk Among Students Attending Seventh-day Adventist Schools in North America." *Journal of School Health,* 68(4): 141–145.

Self-Esteem

Matt recently finished a one-semester course in woodworking. He had never been one to build model airplanes or to fix broken doorknobs for his mother. Matt actually never considered himself to have the skills needed to be considered mechanically inclined or even handy around the house. But his woodworking class was different. He didn't know why, it just was.

Matt felt especially good about the fact that he had fashioned a wooden salad bowl for his mother. When he started this project, he was given several 12″ by 12″ pieces of a dark hardwood. His teacher had him glue each piece together and put large clamps on the pieces so that he ended up with a block—a dark wooden block. It sure didn't look like something that would end up as a bowl, but he followed the teacher's instructions and continued his work.

After the glue had dried and the wood block was ready, his teacher showed him how to attach the block to a lathe. With the lathe on, the block spun around, and as Matt held cutting instruments against the block of wood, chips flew until he could see a large indentation forming. He actually could see how this big chunk of wood would end up on his dinner table full of salad.

Matt liked this project. When the bowl was complete, polished, and cleaned, he proudly took it home and presented it to his mother.

She was thrilled and used it regularly to serve salad.

This simple project gave Matt the sense that he could do something he had previously doubted his ability to accomplish. It felt good! His sense of accomplishment was strengthened. Both Matt's mother and the woodworking teacher praised his excellent work. The woodworking class had improved Matt's self-esteem.

So what is self-esteem? We hear about it all the time. "All kids need is self-esteem and they will do better." Or, "Kids have too much self-esteem. Someone needs to bring them back to reality. They think they rule the world." We hear the term *self-esteem* used so often that many of us have the idea that we really understand what it means. But do we? Let's explore the concept of self-esteem.

Self-esteem is a person's attitude about himself or herself. It's a person's estimation of how capable and worthwhile he or she is. It isn't pride, it isn't conceit, nor is it a boastful, over-inflated opinion about a person's own ability. These things are actually signs of low self-esteem. People with positive self-esteem generally perceive themselves realistically. They understand their strengths and are ready to admit to their weaknesses. People with positive self-esteem do not compare themselves to others or devalue the success of those around them (Joseph, 1994).

You can identify people with positive self-esteem by their ability to make eye contact and to express their feelings and opinions in a polite and appropriate manner. They are likely to take advantage of opportunities to further develop themselves.

Let's contrast two of Matt's classmates, one with positive and the other with negative self-esteem.

Jenny is a great athlete and excellent student. She played on the varsity basketball team and was the playmaker, the spark plug, and the team captain. Jenny could handle the ball with ease. She was fast and made accurate passes. She seemed to be able to score almost any time she wanted to. Jenny was just plain good. And she seemed to handle her status as the team's best quite well until one day a new girl, Vicki, transferred to their school and immediately secured a spot on the team. Vicki could do it all and was even a little better at scoring points than Jenny.

Jenny didn't handle this too well. She claimed that Vicki was a "ball hog" and took too many risky shots. When they lost a game against their school rivals, Jenny blamed the loss on Vicki, claiming that she tried to steal the show and refused to pass when she should have.

Off the basketball court, Jenny often talked about her grades and the fact that she could pick any boy she wanted for a date. She dominated conversations and often tried to change the subject when discussions covered topics out of her range of interest. Jenny didn't smile too much and was not interested in helping others unless there was something in it for her.

Jenny is typical of someone with poor self-esteem. She has all of the tools for success, yet she is classically insecure. She is jealous of other students' achievements, is over-dependent on the approval of others, and is self-centered. Jenny has the makings of a person ready to live an unhappy life throughout her remaining years in high school and as an adult.

Cindy, on the other hand, is well adjusted and secure. She is fairly athletic but doesn't excel at any particular sport. In school, she struggles with reading due to her dyslexia, but she "hangs in there." Cindy tries hard and is satisfied when she gets a C, knowing that she tried her best. Cindy always tries to do her very best in school, is accepted by most of her fellow students, and is never distressed at the successes of her classmates. Her teachers call her a "dream student," though she will never win awards for academic excellence or a scholarship to college.

When Cindy starts a project, she doesn't stop until it is completed. When things don't come out the way she wants, she isn't demoralized because she is confident that she did the best that she could. Cindy doesn't choose friends because of their status, and she is a friend of nearly everyone. She does not require the approval of everyone around her. Cindy's self-esteem is very positive.

Jenny has more basic ability and natural talents than does Cindy. Yet Cindy's potential for success and productivity are greater than Jenny's. Cindy has what researchers refer to as a "productive personality" (Joseph, 1994). She is self-motivated, self-assured, persistent, and responsible. She is not stunted with worries about how she compares to others or how much adulation she needs from others. Because she is generally well regarded by her peers and teachers, she gets a lot of positive feedback that further fuels her positive self-esteem. Because schoolwork is a challenge, she has had to learn good study skills and a strong work ethic. These two things will remain with her for life.

So where does self-esteem come from? Can we teach our kids to have it? Should we develop a self-esteem program for our schools so that all students can emerge with positive self-esteem? Well, let's see if we can identify where self-esteem comes from.

Cooley, a psychologist, described self-esteem as something that comes from the feedback, real or imagined, we receive from others. He suggested that we tend to value ourselves the same way that we believe other people value us. He referred to this as the "looking glass self" (Joseph, 1994). It has been proposed that children have fairly well-developed self-esteem, whether it be positive or negative, by the time they reach eight years of age.

If self-esteem comes from others, it only makes sense that we must have "others" around us in order to develop positive self-esteem. If we grow up in a socially isolated environment where we have little contact with other people—especially with adults—it is logical that we may not have the opportunity to develop a positive self-esteem unless our parent or parents are adept at pointing out our true strengths and reinforcing our successes. We aren't talking about a parent or parents who endlessly tell kids that they are the best, better than others, and do everything well. Kids are not fools. They can see right through transparent praise.

So, you might ask, who is growing up in a socially isolated environment in today's world? Many—maybe most—kids are, possibly your own. The lives of parents are often so busy that they spend very few moments each week in meaningful conversation with their own kids. That is social isolation. But, you might argue, how about church? Don't kids get enough attention from adults at church? The answer to this is probably a sad but resounding "no."

It is typical in Christian churches today for the church leaders to search endlessly, often begging, for adults to spend time with kids in Sabbath or Sunday school. It seems as though the few adults who agree to assist in kindergarten in church are the same few people year after year. One of the toughest challenges of nominating committees in churches is the chore of locating adults willing to spend time with kids in what are sometimes called the "divisions."

Further, how many adults in your church even know the names of every youngster who attends church? Where can young people get the sense that they are valued if no one pays attention to them or even calls them by name? Sadly, social isolation is often prevalent even in church.

Another psychologist, Maslow, postulated that self-esteem is necessary for a person to be truly productive. He suggested that we get self-esteem from the love, respect, and acceptance that we get from others (Joseph, 1994). It seems clear that we need others in our lives in order to have self-esteem.

Researchers have tried to teach self-esteem to students in school. In two schools, they did self-esteem tests on the students before they started their program. In one school the students did self-esteem-enhancing activities each morning. In the other school, they did nothing different and didn't even discuss self-esteem with the students.

The self-esteem-enhancing exercises included having the students spend five minutes each morning, the first five minutes in class, talking to themselves about how good they were, how they were doing well, and on and on. At the end of several months of doing these exercises, self-esteem tests were performed again on both schools. After an analysis of the data, they found there was no difference in the self-esteem of the students in either school. The reason that this didn't work is that you don't teach yourself to have high self-esteem nor is self-esteem taught to you. That's not how you get it. As Maslow suggested, we get it from others.

If you were to test Matt's self-esteem, you would probably find it to be fairly positive. Remember, Matt isn't a stellar athlete or academic all-star. He is an average kid who gets C's and B's in school. He has been told that he has dyslexia, similar to Cindy, which means that the letters of words seem to scramble in is head and this makes reading somewhat difficult. Matt isn't terribly fond of the term *dyslexia*. He thinks it sounds like a disease. He is satisfied that he tries hard and seems to have a little trouble reading. No big deal to him.

One of Matt's sources of self-esteem comes from his mother. If you recall, she spends a few moments every evening talking with him about his day. She encourages him in a gentle but loving way, cautions him about some of the decisions he will have to make regarding drugs, sex, etc., and assures him in both a spoken and non-spoken way that her love for him is unconditional. He is reassured that he can always come to her to talk about anything, even if he has done something that he shouldn't have.

Matt also gets self-esteem from his Uncle Vanny, the guy with the big belly who went out with the family for ice cream. Matt's father lives a couple of thousand miles away, and though he calls often, their relationship has been difficult to take to a level that Matt would ideally hope for. Uncle Vanny is "way cool." He comes by the house a couple of times each week just to say hi to Matt and his sister. Matt and his uncle sometimes go out for a soft drink or maybe go fishing. Uncle Vanny's consistent presence in Matt's life has been a source of strength for him. Uncle Vanny is a guy who Matt could go to for an answer to even the most sensitive question.

It is interesting that the New Testament provides a concrete example of the way in which two leaders in the early church helped a young man survive and develop into one of the gospel writers. John Mark (Marcus in Latin) was raised in the home of the "upper room" in Jerusalem, where for some time at least the apostles lived after the Christ's resurrection and ascension. He accompanied Paul and Barnabas on their first missionary trip, but, becoming homesick, he left them at Pamphylia. Paul viewed this as "deserting them" (Acts 15:37-39) and refused to take him a second time.

But Barnabas, his cousin, gave the young man another chance and took John Mark with him. This mentoring increased John Mark's confidence, so that he was able to become a translator for another apostle, Peter. Peter, another mentor, speaks of John Mark as "his son" (1 Peter 5:13). John Mark is generally regarded as the writer of the earliest gospel, called by his name. From "deserter" to gospel writer, John Mark demonstrates the powerful influence of people who care, who grant acceptance and support.

So, how do we give our children and even those around us positive self-esteem? We give the unconditional positive acceptance. To do this, we need to focus on loving them rather than judging them based on their behaviors or academic successes. In order to make this happen, it is essential to spend quality time with them on a regular basis. This doesn't mean to smother them with undeserved adulation but take twenty minutes a day, three or four times each week, to talk, to listen, and to enjoy their company.

It is important that young people not see us as "sacrificing" our time in order to mechanically pay attention to them. They need to have the sense that we have an honest interest in them and that we are able to put aside our duties or chores because of the genuine interest we have in their lives. Showering kids with gifts does not communicate to them that they are valued. What is important is quality time spent. It is also important for young people to know with certainty that we are interested in what they are doing (Joseph, 1994).

Children need to know where their strengths and weaknesses lie. They learn some of this through trial and error. But much of it comes because a parent or other adult spends time with them and takes the opportunity to identify what they have done well. And it is equally important to assist them by pointing out what might have been done better or maybe what they do not have an apparent talent for. When a child acts responsibly, this needs to be reinforced. If Matt was your child or a member of your church you might say, "Matt, I really appreciate the fact that you always follow through. When you say you are going to do something, I admire you for sticking to it until it is done. I really like that about you."

On the other hand, you might be a neighbor who is a nuclear physicist and Matt holds you up as a mentor or role model. In his interactions with you he might mention that he is taking physics in high school because he wants to grow up to be like you. But in his class he is struggling miserably. It may be that Matt just doesn't have an aptitude for physics. It would be your responsibility not to tell him that he will never make it in the world of physics but rather to find his strengths and guide him into those areas where he could find more satisfaction and success.

None of the interactions needed to cultivate positive self-esteem in young people can happen if they don't have adults in their lives who are willing to spend time with them and love them unconditionally. And it really doesn't take a lot of time.

This is the key: *When you are at church this next weekend, pick out a few young people and learn their names.* Walk up to them with a smile, one at a time, greet them by name, and ask them how their week went.

At first, they may feel somewhat awkward, as they really don't know you. But hang in there. Do it again and again from one weekend to the next. Eventually they will start coming to you just to chat for a moment. They will come to you because they enjoy friendly people; they like to be cared for.

Eventually you will get to know them well enough to know how life is really going for them. You will learn their struggles, and this will place you in a position to offer a few moments of your time to assist them in areas that you may never have thought of had you not learned their names and cultivated a caring relationship.

In order for kids to develop positive self-esteem, they need other people in their lives. Parents are certainly essential, but other adults matter tremendously. You can make a difference in the lives of young people, and it won't take much effort on your part.

So kids need knowledge and information. But this probably won't be sufficient to solve their problems. They also need significant adults in their lives in order to develop a sense that they have value. They need to have people to whom they can turn for questions, sometimes very sensitive ones, and unless you have a well-established relationship with them, they won't even know that they could go to you for assistance.

Is this all you need to know? Probably not.

Joseph , J. M. (1994). *The Resilient Child.* Chapter 1: Self-esteem. Plenum Press: New York.

Social Support

When Matt was younger, his grandfather had a stroke and because he needed long- term nursing care, he was admitted to a nursing home two blocks away from Matt's home. Matt and his grandfather were very close and had spent a lot of quality time together as long as he could remember.

Matt was troubled about his grandfather's new and sudden disability. Gramps had a hard time talking, couldn't walk at all, and sat in his wheelchair with his head hanging down staring at the floor for hours. This wasn't the same man that Matt had spent so many hours with.

Because of his affection for his grandfather, Matt stopped by to see Gramps almost every day, often for just a few minutes in the afternoon after school and regularly with his mother on weekends. Though his grandfather couldn't express himself clearly, Matt could tell that Gramps was happy to see him.

Matt recalls that every time he walked into the nursing home, there was a nice lady who always sat in her wheelchair next to the nursing station. Matt didn't know what was wrong with her, but she was very quiet. Her left leg was all wrapped up with a splint and stuck straight out of the wheelchair. She seemed sad even with no noticeable expression on her face.

One weekend when Matt and his mom were visiting Gramps, a nurse came into the room to give his grandfather some medication.

Matt asked the nurse what was wrong with the lady who always sat next to the nursing station in the wheelchair. The nurse explained that the lady's name was Miss Rae, and that she was a retired school teacher. She had slipped and fallen in her icy driveway the previous winter, maybe six or seven months ago. In the spill she had suffered a very serious fracture to bones in her leg, had undergone several operations, and the injury had left her in severe pain and unable to walk.

The next time Matt was at the nursing home, he stopped in front of Miss Rae, got down on one knee, looked her in the eyes and said, "Hi, Miss Rae, my name is Matt." She didn't react much except to say "Hi" very quietly. Matt made it a point to stop and greet Miss Rae every time he went to see Gramps.

One day, Matt stooped down to say hi, and he noticed something different. Miss Rae actually looked into his eyes and smiled. This time she said, "Hello, Matt." It was such a little thing, but it made him feel good. As the days passed and Matt continued to greet Miss Rae, each time her smile grew and her greetings became friendlier. Maybe she was just getting more comfortable with him.

One day, Miss Rae stopped Matt and asked him how old he was, what grade he was in school, about his family. She just seemed to want to talk. Matt was a little surprised by her interest, but he pulled up a chair and talked with her for ten or fifteen minutes. Miss Rae was really nice.

Matt stopped one of the nurses one afternoon and inquired about Miss Rae. He wondered why he had never seen her with any other people. Didn't she have any family who visited her? The nurse explained that Miss Rae's family lived right there in town but visited her only occasionally. They really didn't spend much time with her. They seemed nice but apparently were very busy with their own lives.

Matt and Miss Rae developed a great friendship. She told him that she wished that she could still get around on her own so that she could bake cookies for him. Matt understood.

The nurse stopped Matt in the hallway one afternoon and asked him if he realized how much difference he had made in Miss Rae's recovery. He didn't understand. She explained that Miss Rae's doctor had recently asked the nurse what had happened. Miss Rae was using less pain medication, and her physical therapist reported that the treatments on her leg had shown much progress. Miss Rae would soon be walking with assistance.

How could a simple greeting that led to the friendly relationship between Miss Rae and Matt actually lead to improvement in her recovery? What was the connection between his being nice and Miss Rae needing less pain medication? Maybe it was just coincidental. Maybe Miss Rae was improving on her own and Matt's kindness had nothing to do with it.

A study reported at the 1997 Clinical Congress of the American College of Surgeons, however, revealed that actual impairment accounts for only 23% of patients' continuing dysfunction a year after treatment for trauma to a leg. More important to the patients' recovery is the presence of adequate *social support.* "People with better social support networks had better recovery even given the same pain and the same level of injury" (Key & DeNoon, 1997). Matt had been the social support that Miss Rae had needed. His kindness and willingness to be a friend had made a difference, a positive difference, in her recovery. Matt's caring, or *love,* had helped Miss Rae's healing. Does that sound far-fetched? It isn't.

Social support is an emotion-based attachment between two or more people. It is simply a meaningful relationship. When you get to know individuals, when you call them by name and ask how they are doing, you become a friend, and good things begin to happen. They will actually benefit emotionally and become healthier physically. If they are already healthy, maybe you will be helping them to stay healthy. Your willingness to form a relationship will not make them perfect, but it will give them strength.

A 1997 report described research on social support and drug use among high school students (Weinrich & Hardin). What the researchers explored was whether social support was related to drug use in their sample of students. They learned that students who had low social support used more drugs than those with higher social support. This research didn't describe that students with high social support suddenly became perfect, but rather they improved in their ability to avoid drugs. Social support, or relationships with others, particularly adults, is part of what kids need in their difficult journey through the troubled waters of life. Having people around them who care makes them stronger and more resilient; they are more able to survive and do well in spite of the heavy odds against their success in life.

We heard about a community (this is not a scientific study using strict rules of research) in the Northwest where alcohol and teen pregnancy surfaced as a problem. The school board was concerned about the kids and would often hold town meetings to discuss what to do.

They started with the logical steps. They consulted with experts in teen pregnancy and spent thousands of dollars on the purchase of a packaged teen-pregnancy-reduction program. It looked great. The packets that came with the purchase of the program included colorful texts as well as professionally produced and edited videos. The actors portrayed in the videos were famous and recognizable, the same ones that the kids had seen in the movies. This was great. How could it miss? The kids loved it and often talked about how neat it was and told their parents how much they enjoyed it. The school board, which had been reluctant to spend thousands of dollars on the purchase of this highly acclaimed program, saw the reaction of the kids and they thought they had found an effective means to reduce teen pregnancy. They really worried about their kids and wanted to be able to help them. Finally they had found something that looked like it would work!

After a full year of the teen-pregnancy-prevention education, the students remained enthusiastic. Interest had not diminished. The kids really liked this program. One of the items that they liked the most was that the program came with fancy dolls. These dolls were life-like, weighed about the same as an infant, and had clothing along with hair that was realistic. The dolls had little computers installed to make them cry and even wet their diapers at timed intervals. The teacher would program the doll and give one to each of the students to carry to class and take home for two full weeks.

The students were required to carry the their babies (dolls) to class and take them home every day. Part of the assignment was that when the students went out, even after school hours, they had to take the dolls with them. Along with the doll they had to take a bag with dry diapers, liquid that looked like baby formula in a real baby bottle, and a bag with towels and other items necessary for a parent with a real infant.

The dolls would cry at intervals just as a baby would. In order to stop this loud shriek, the student had to have a key handy to insert into the proper place to stop the crying. The students would wake up two or three times every night to change diapers, feed their babies, or stop the crying. This was very real.

The school liked this program so much that they purchased it for a second year, and again the students seemed to really enjoy it. They especially looked forward to the part of the class when they were assigned their own babies to feed and care for.

After two years, the school board met and an alert teacher asked a critical question. "I know how much the kids like the teen pregnancy prevention program, but I wonder if it has really worked. I wonder if fewer teen pregnancies have occurred since we started this program." The registrar was asked to review the records of how many young girls had dropped out of school for the past five years. She would also do some investigative work to see if she could identify how many of the dropouts were due to pregnancy.

At the next school board meeting the registrar reported the rates of teen pregnancy over the past five years seemed to be stable. The number of girls in that school who had quit due to pregnancy hadn't changed. The board members just stared at each other for a few minutes. They were really surprised. The kids had enjoyed the program. Why hadn't it made a difference?

After the pause, a rancher, wearing cowboy boots with his feet propped up on a chair said, "I don't know what to do. It seems like when I was a kid, everyone in town knew us, called us by name, and sort of hooked into our lives. People were real back then, and these problems weren't very common. Maybe we should get to know these kids." Board members reminisced about their earlier days and then someone came up with an idea. "Let's hold a town meeting. There are only about twelve hundred people living here. Let's ask every adult in town to learn the names of every kid. Let's greet them every time we see them and get to know them. Maybe that will have a better effect than our expensive curriculum." The board members weren't overwhelmed with the idea but decided to give it a try. They presented the idea at the next town meeting. The townspeople seemed willing to try it. What did they have to lose? It wouldn't cost anything.

So, this plan was put into place. When old Abe saw a kid at the store, he would stop for a second and ask his name. "Hey, I've seen you around but don't know what to call you. What's your name?" "My name is Mike." "Nice to know you Mike," Abe responded. "Call me Abe."

After that is seemed simple, "Hi, Mike." "Hi Abe." Nothing to it. One afternoon Abe came out of the hardware store, and there stood Mike with a beer can in his hand. Abe said, "Hi, Mike." Mike quickly put the beer can behind his back. He didn't know why but he felt nervous holding a beer with Abe looking at him. Mike was uncomfortable and Abe could tell. Something had happened. Just by Abe learning Mike's name, a relationship had started. With that relationship came a little bit of commitment. Mike didn't want to disappoint Abe; he seemed so nice. Abe didn't scold Mike; he actually didn't say a thing. He simply smiled, as always, and went on with his business.

Several months after the town started on their effort to learn the names of the local kids, they had another town meeting. There was an enthusiastic buzz in the room. People couldn't wait to tell their stories; every person in the room seemed to have one. People told of the relationships they had developed with youngsters in town that started just by learning their names.

Two years later, at a school board meeting the registrar mentioned something interesting. "It looks like the number of school dropouts has decreased for some reason. I did some digging of my own, and it actually looks like the number of girls who quit school due to pregnancy has decreased." There were still a few pregnancies among the students but improvement was obvious. "Do you think that this has something to do with the townspeople learning the names of the kids?"

What happened in that little town shows the benefit of social support, relationships developed just by learning the names of the kids. It was starting to show in the reduced numbers of high-school-aged girls who were getting pregnant. The chief of police mentioned that the number of arrests for drug use among young people also had decreased in the previous two years.

Social support, relationships with others, a network of people who care, or *love* is very powerful. And it doesn't take much effort or cost any money!

The biblical story of Esther illustrates what social support can do. Esther—without father or mother and living as a young woman exiled in a foreign land—was raised by her cousin Mordecai. Even after she was chosen to go to the palace during King Xerxes's search for a new queen, "she continued to follow Mordecai's instruction as she had done when he was bringing her up" (Esther 2:20, NIV). When disaster threatened her and all of her people with death, she replied to Mordecai's appeal with the message to gather all of the Jews in Susa to fast, just as she and her maidens would do. Empowered by that network of social support, she vowed, " 'I will go to the king, even though it is against the law. And if I perish, I perish' " (Esther 4:16,17, NIV). The results of her bravery are described in the remainder of the book of Esther.

An abundance of research in the past two decades reveals the benefits of social support. It seems that the power of love expressed through caring relationships carries health benefits beyond reducing drug use or teen pregnancy. Here are some of the findings:

- College students who report high levels of social support also report significantly lower levels of stress (Ainslie & Shafer, 1996).
- Larger social networks are related to fewer hospitalizations (Albert, Becker, McCrone, & Thornicroft, 1998).
- Social support and spirituality empowers older adults for sustained practice of health-promoting activities (Boland, 1998).
- A caring adult or supportive peer relationship can serve as a buffer to the experience of childhood physical abuse (Milner, 1989).
- Low social support is associated with a greater chance of death during the recovery phase following heart attack (Farmer, & Meter, 1996).
- When Hispanic female college students believed that their university environment was friendly and supportive, and they perceived social support from friends, they dropped out of college less often (Gloria, 1997).
- Patients with breast cancer and patients with a serious, life-threatening skin cancer (melanoma) survive longer when they have social support (Maunsell, Brisson, &Deschenes, 1995).
- Chronically ill women with social support (love from others) have less depression (Hough, & Brumitt, 1999).
- Social support is associated with improved performance on aca-

demic examinations (Goldsmith, & Albrecht, 1993).

- Social support for abused adolescent mothers predicts higher birth weight babies as compared to those with low social support (Lindgren, 1999).
- Lack of social support is associated with problem behaviors (drug and alcohol use, delinquent acts) among youth. Strong social support attenuates this adverse effect (McCreary, & Slavine, 1996).
- Social support is often less present in the lives of youth who are at risk of school failure (Rickman & Rosenfled, 1998).
- Students who report no or low-support have lower attendance, spend less time studying, have fewer prosocial (positive) behaviors, and have less ability to overcome school problems. Those with low support from their families engage in less disclosure of their feelings with the adults with whom they live; also, they report that their adult caretakers show less interest in their school and monitor school activities less (Rosenfled, & Rickman, 1998).
- Social support is associated with successful vocational outcomes among individuals who have suffered a brain injury (Kaplan, 1988).
- Teenage mothers who have support from family members, friends, and the father of the child pursue educational and career goals more often (Kissman, 1990).
- Teenage mothers who have social support are only slightly less likely to graduate from high school than those who do not become mothers as teens (Sells & Blum, 1996).

Social support, or love, is health giving. "For social support to be effective, it must be embedded in emotion-based attachment" (Rosenthal, 1995). Sincere, honest relationships promote good health.

What Matt learned from his experience with Miss Rae was that being nice and taking an interest in other people actually yields measurable benefits. Miss Rae is now living at home, and though she needs a walker to get around, she is caring for herself again. She enjoys making cookies for Matt; they are still friends.

What we can learn from research on social support is that it is our duty to become involved in the lives of others. It is more important than donating money, though there are many causes that need funding. The work of preventing drug use and teen pregnancy among kids or helping to promote survival among people with cancer is ours—every one of us.

Knowledge is very important, but knowledge alone isn't enough. Self-esteem is important, but in order to develop it we need others in our lives to love and encourage us. Social support is certainly self-esteem enhancing. But, is all of this enough? Well, we are getting close, but read on!

Ainslie, R. C., and A. Shafer. 1996. "Mediators of Adolescents' Stress in a College Preparatory Environment." *Adolescence, 31*(124): 913–926.

Albert, M., T. Becker, P. Mccrone., and G. Thornicroft. 1998. "Social Networks and Mental Health Service Utilization—a Literature Review." *International Journal of Social Psychiatry, 44*(4): 248–258.

Boland, C. 1998. "Parish Nursing." *Journal of Holistic Nursing, 16*(3): 355–68.

Farmer, I. P., and P. S. Meter. 1996. "Higher Levels of Social Support Predict Greater Survival Following Acute Myocardial Infarction: The Corpus Cristi Heart Project." *Behavioral Medicine, 2*(59): 59–67.

Gloria, A. M. 1997. "Chicana Academic Persistence." *Education and Urban Society, 30*(1): 107–121.

Goldsmith, D., and T. L Albrecht. 1993. "The Impact of Supportive Communication Networks on Test Anxiety and Performance." *Communication Education, 42*: 142–158.

Hough, E. S., and G. A. Brumitt,. 1999. "Social Support, Demands of Illness, and Depression in Chronically Ill Urban Women." *Health Care for Women International, 20*(4): 349–462.

Kaplan, S. 1988. "Adaptation Following Serious Brain Injury: An Assessment After One Year." *Journal of Applied Rehabilitation Counseling, 19*: 3–8.

Key, S. W., and D. J. DeNoon,. 1997. "Social Support Improved Recovery for Patients With Traumatic Injury." *Disease Weekly Plus* (10/27/97): 18–19.

Kissman, K. 1990. "Social Support and Gender Role Attitude Among Teenage Mothers." *Adolescence 25*(99): 709–717.

Lindgren, M. August 1999. "Support Attenuates Abuse Effects in Adolescent Mothers." *World Disease Weekly Plus* (8/16/99): 4, 5.

Maunsell, E., J. Brisson,and L. Deschenes. 1995. "Social Support and Survival Among Women With Breast Cancer." *Cancer* 76(4) (August 15, 1995): 631–637.

McCreary, M. L. and L. A. Slavine. 1996. "Predicting Problem Behavior and Self-esteem Among African-American Adolescents." *Journal of Adolescent Health Research, 11*(2): 216–234.

Milner, J. S. 1989. "Additional Cross-validation of the Child Abuse Potential Inventory." *Psychological Assessment: A Journal of Consulting and Clinical Psychology, 1*: 219–223.

Rickman, J. M., and L. B. Rosenfled, et al. 1998. "Social Support for Adolescents at Risk of School Failure" *Social Work, 43*(4): 309–423.

Rosenfeld, L. R., and J. M. Richman. 1998. "Low Social Support Among At-risk Adolescents." *Social Work in Education, 20*(4): 245–259.

Rosenthal, B. S. 1995. "The Influence of Social Support on School Completion Among Haitians." *Social Work in Education17*(1): 30–39.

Sells, C. W., and Blum, R. W. 1996. "Current Trends in Adolescent Health." In *Handbook of Adolescent Health Risk Behaviors*. Eds. R. J., DiClemente, W. B. Hansen, and L. Ponton, New York: Plenum Press.

Weinrich, S., and S. Hardin. 1997. "Social Support and Psychological Correlates of High School Students Who Use Illicit Drugs in Response to Stress." *American Journal of Health Studies 13*(1): 17–26.

Resilience

Jenny left the court after the team just barely won a basketball game against a really tough opponent. It was close until the end, but Cindy sank a three-point shot just before the buzzer. What a great victory! Jenny wished she had been the one to score the winning points. The girls on the team swarmed around Cindy and jumped up and down, screaming at the top of their lungs. For Jenny, the joy of winning was mixed with a little jealousy.

Matt's focus was on Jenny—those dimples! He was glad that his team had won, but as usual, he couldn't take his eyes off Jenny. She didn't join the rest of the team in their celebration, which puzzled Matt. He didn't spend a lot of time thinking about it as he watched Jenny walk off of the court, leaving her team behind. No one else seemed to notice.

Matt stopped to talk with a couple of buddies before he left the gymnasium. On his way out, he saw Jenny standing on the sidewalk alone. She looked like she was waiting for someone. He walked over to her and congratulated her on the victory. Jenny didn't say much, but she did smile. From some unknown place deep in Matt's chest, he suddenly organized the courage to ask her if she wanted to go across the street and get a soda. Jenny looked a little surprised but spontaneously said, "Sure." Neither of them expected their rides for another twenty minutes or so.

The two of them talked about the game and Matt could tell that Jenny was a little uncomfortable about something. He wasn't sure what it was. He was just happy to get to spend a few moments with her. After finishing their sodas, they went back to the gym where both of their mothers arrived at just about the same moment. Jenny thanked Matt for the drink, and they both went home.

Matt was really excited. In his wildest dream he had never thought that Jenny would spend even a moment with him alone. But she did! He had a little difficulty falling asleep that night.

The next day was a typical day at school. Matt saw Jenny a few times, and they talked a little bit. No real big deal, but sort of exciting for him.

After about a week of short chats and friendly greetings, Matt noticed that Jenny looked like she enjoyed seeing him. He occasionally caught her looking at him in class—then she would quickly return her attention to the teacher. One afternoon he asked Jenny if she would mind if he called her sometime. She smiled, looked like she was glad that he had asked, and gave him her phone number. "This is a private line to my room," she said.

She's lucky! She has her own phone. Her parents must be rich, Matt thought. He could hardly wait to get home, finish dinner, and give Jenny a call. Maybe this was the start of something great. He really wondered what was going through her mind.

He called and, sure enough, she was home and seemed to enjoy the short conversation. They didn't talk about anything terribly important, just chatted. Hey, it was a start. He felt pretty good about it. At the end of the phone conversation Matt heard a male voice say, "Jenny, get off the phone, put your nose in a book, and do it now." Matt's mother had never talked to him that way. Jenny ended the call with a quick, "Gotta go."

As they became better friends, Matt learned that Jenny came from a home where her parents were divorced, just as his parents were. Her father lived locally but had a new girlfriend and didn't spend too much time with Jenny. Her mom had then married a well-known attorney in town. Her stepdad was quite successful. Money was no issue in their family. They seemed to have everything.

Matt learned that Jenny's stepfather was very demanding, much as her real father had been. He drove her to study and excel at everything.

He demanded perfection, not only from her but of her mother, as well. The night that Jenny's team won their game at the last minute, her stepfather asked if she had scored the most points. He didn't seem to pay attention to the fact that they had won; it was her personal achievement that he focused on. Jenny vowed to herself that she would somehow have to become better than Cindy and regain the status of being the high scorer on the team.

One evening on the phone, Matt asked Jenny why she seemed so low. She asked him if he could come over, as she needed to talk. Wow, he couldn't wait. Matt's mom drove him over to Jenny's home, and they sat on the front lawn and talked. Her parents were home but had company. Jenny told her story, sometimes tearfully. She recalled how her real father used to scream at her; sometimes he beat her with his hand or a belt. He insisted that Jenny was stupid and wouldn't ever make anything out of life. All she ever did was wrong. He treated her mother the same way, and that led to the divorce.

Jenny's mom had remarried into a similar situation only at least her stepfather had money. In her new home she didn't get hit anymore, but she was often ridiculed for not performing perfectly. "Don't ever let anyone do better than you," she was admonished. During her eighth- and ninth-grade years, she had been sent home twice for acting out in class. Both times her stepfather scolded her with the same remark, "Look what you have done to us. You are an embarrassment. People will think we are bad parents." There was no attention given to Jenny's feelings.

She told Matt about her older sister Jill, who at the age of 18 was fed up with the whole drill. She quit school, left home, and was living somewhere on the streets of San Francisco. Last Jenny had heard, Jill was pregnant and after living alone for several months, she ended up moving in with an older man who was abusive.

Jenny admitted that she often thought of leaving as her sister had. But it looked to her as though the pain she was suffering at home was better than the pains that Jill was suffering. Jenny's strategy was to hang in there, try to satisfy her demanding stepfather, and put up with the endless harassment until she could make a life of her own.

Matt just listened. He didn't realize that there were real people living like this. He had seen it on TV and in the movies but had never met anyone who had to live under so much pressure with so little care or love. He didn't know just what to do, but he softly reassured Jenny saying, "You know, you are doing pretty well in spite of what is going on around you. You seem to have every reason to give up but you don't." After all, her grades were nearly perfect, although still not good enough for her stepdad, but much better than Matt ever expected to do in his wildest dreams. Also, she was nearly the best player on her basketball team.

Jenny said, "If you think I've beaten the odds, you should hear Elizabeth's story." Elizabeth, or Lizzie as known to her classmates, grew up in a home where her parents were both alcoholics. There were parties, fights, and constant chaos. Lizzie's parents would invite in a few friends for a night of drugs and booze, and if she got scared and cried, they would lock her in a closet for hours. During one three-day binge, her parents actually chained her to her bed. Eventually the police stepped in, and Lizzie was sent to live with foster parents. That was even worse. Her foster father sexually assaulted her and beat her endlessly. Again, the authorities were called in, and Lizzie was relocated, this time to a very caring and kind family who eventually adopted her.

Over time, with the constant love of her new family, Lizzie started to become more trusting and sort of "came out of her shell," as Jenny described. Matt was shocked. Lizzie was an excellent student, never seemed to miss class, one of the most popular kids in their class, and seemed like she had everything in the world going for her. Lizzie was truly a survivor. She was a picture of resilience.

Later, after Matt had a few days to think about Jenny's situation, he asked her if there was anyone at all in her life to whom she could go to for reassurance. Jenny explained that her mom certainly wasn't that person. Her mother was pretty much a puppet to her stepfather. When Jenny had gone to her in the past, her mom would only say, "Just a few more years, and you will leave for college. Your stepfather is a great provider. Just excel at everything you do, and try to say out of his path."

Jenny then described her grandmother, Betty. Jenny called her GrannyB. She had moved to town just weeks after Jill left home. GrannyB and Jenny had bonded. She talked to Jenny about how special she was. She was kind, thoughtful, and willing to chat any time. Jenny felt accepted unconditionally for the first time in her life. GrannyB was really neat.

Jenny and Lizzie were both resilient. Their stories were quite different although somewhat similar. Both had stressors in their lives that challenged them, both had suffered abuse though Lizzie's was more severe, and both seemed to have better reasons to give up than to forge ahead.

Behavioral research typically looks at what puts young people at risk for their involvement in risky behaviors. Recently, a new and powerful concept has arisen that has inspired hope among researchers and educators; it is the concept of *resilience*. Resilience is the capacity to maintain competent functioning in spite of adversity or life stressors. Resilience appears to develop over time as a result of environmental support (Kaplan, & Turner, S. et al., 1996). Resilient individuals are those who, despite severe hardships and the presence of at-risk factors, develop characteristics of coping skills that enable them to succeed in life (Kaplan, & Turner, S. et al., 1996).

Researchers have explained resilience in terms of hardiness, and suggested that resilient individuals have a strong commitment to self and/or their God and are willing to take action and deal with problems. They also have a positive attitude toward their environment, hold a strong sense of purpose, and develop a strong internal strength that enables them to see life's obstacles as challenges that can be overcome (Herbert, 1996). Resiliency seems to be all about hope; it is the sense that adversity can be overcome, that there is life beyond the obstacles of today.

Rather than focusing on the shortcomings of young people who are at risk of academic failure, drug use, or other at-risk behaviors, the resilience idea attempts to identify factors that account for success (Gonzalez, R. & Padilla, M, 1997). Resilient youth often have the ability to use their religious faith to maintain a positive vision of a meaningful life (Herbert, 1996).

Most of us have read that children who are sexually or physically abused, those like Lizzie who are raised in homes where the parents are alcoholics, or kids who face severe hardship during their developmental years, are at great risk for poor social, behavioral, or academic outcomes. However, not all of these young people emerge scathed. Some do well. Resiliency research identifies what is associated with success in spite of some of these terrible situations.

The concept of resilience would inspire us to ask an important question. If we can't get Matt's and Jenny's school to become perfect—which we know is unlikely—if we can't get the drugs off the street, if we can't get violence off the television, movies, and video games, and if we can't get the filth off the Internet, how can we help kids who grow up exposed to all of these influences still do well? How can kids grow up exposed to seven hours and fifteen minutes per day of electronic media and still do well?

A careful review of the available research of what fosters resilience among young people, one important influencing factor emerges repeatedly. That factor is valuable, sincere, and enduring relationships.

Supportive older adults, mentors ranging from teachers to clergy, may contribute to resilience among youth (Herbert, 1996). From studies conducted around the world, researchers have identified a number of factors that enable children of misfortune to beat the heavy odds against them. One factor turns out to be the presence in their lives of a charismatic adult—a person with whom they identify and from whom they gather strength (Brooks, 1994).

Relationships with individuals who provide care, warmth, and unconditional love appear to provide young people with a sense that the odds they face in life can be overcome. These relationships appear to provide youngsters with self-esteem and a sense of self-worth that makes successful coping more likely. One study found that "resilient youngsters all had at least one person in their lives that accepted them unconditionally, regardless of temperamental idiosyncrasies, physical attractiveness, or intelligence" (Brooks, 1994).

Resilience to the stressors of life such as drug abusing peers, media violence, or the influence of a less than ideal home appears to come through *supportive relationships*!

Think again about what Matt, Jenny, and Lizzie face every day at school. Sometimes students carry weapons, most students have used alcohol and many binge drink, drug use is extremely common, and of course there is the all-pervasive influence of the media. These kids have a lot going against them. They need to become resilient.

The Bible provides an illustration of a lad who, though he grew up with some very bad examples of behavior on the part of church leaders, possessed resilience. Samuel had been given to the temple because his mother felt that he was a gift of God in answer to her prayer (1 Samuel 1:19-29). She visited him only once a year, bringing him a robe she had made when she and her husband went to make their annual offering. Eli, the high priest, had done a very poor job of raising his sons, Hophni and Phinehas. With the continued example of stealing and prostitution, with little guidance from Eli, and only a yearly visit from his mother, Samuel had everything in his environment going against him. But, he was attuned to what the Lord had said, with the result that the Bible records, "The Lord was with Samuel as he grew up, and he let none of his words fall to the ground" (1 Samuel 3:19). Talk about resilience!

Remember, we don't teach a kid how to become resilient. We educate them and give them knowledge, which we know alone won't solve the problems that they face. We surround them with social support or a loving and caring environment, we learn their names and greet them personally taking a few moments to talk one-on-one, and we develop enduring relationships with them. Through these steps, they build strength and improve their ability to defeat the overwhelming odds they face every single day.

Brooks, R. 1994. "Children at Risk: Fostering Resilience and Hope." *American Journal of Orthopsychiatry,* 64(4): 545–553.

Gonzalez, R., and M. Padilla. 1997. "The Academic Resilience of Mexican American High School Students." *Hispanic Journal of Behavioral Sciences, 19*(3) (August): 310–318.

Herbert, T. P. 1996. "Portraits of Resilience: The Urban Life Experience of Gifted Latino Young Men." *Roeper Review, 19*(2)(December): 82–91.

Kaplan, C. P., and S. Turner, et al. 1996. "Promoting Resilience Strategies: A Modified Consultation Model." *Social Work in Education, 18*(3)(July): 158–161.

Communication and Sex

Matt hears about sex every day of his life. Most of his classmates are sexually experienced. At school, sex is one of the most common topics among his peers. Television and movies are full of sexual scenes and innuendos. On the Internet, a huge number of pornography sites are only a mouse click away. He couldn't get away from sex talk if he wanted to. It's everywhere.

Though Matt is not sexually experienced—in other words, he has never had sexual intercourse—he finds the shapes of young girls to be appealing and interesting, he likes to look at girls, and he often wonders how it would feel to touch one of them. Quite simply, Matt has sexual interests and urges. After all, he has sex hormones just as do his teachers, his parents, and all of the adults in his world.

It doesn't seem right that someone only fifteen years of age should have to face all of this. Sex is a powerful urge. Shouldn't it be reserved for adults who supposedly have greater power to resist such temptations? What has happened so that the very young are thrown into a world so driven by sex?

It may seem like these sexual interests are occurring at younger ages than ever before. Let's take a look at what has happened regarding sex and youth. Doesn't it seem like more kids are having sex than ever before? The answer is yes. Why? Are the sexual urges different from those in years past, or what's happening here?

Biologically, young women start to feel sexual feelings shortly after they experience their first menstrual period. When we look back into the eighteenth century, we find that girls didn't have their first period until they were sixteen or seventeen years of age. Since that time, the age of the first period has steadily decreased. Today, the typical age at which a young girl has her first period is 12.8 years, many times even earlier than that. So, here we have young girls, elementary school age, starting to recognize that they are becoming more interested in boys, often boys who are older, sometimes much older than they are (Kreipe & Sahler, 1991).

Women in the eighteenth century sensed their first sexual interests when they were in the stage of development called late adolescence. Typically, late adolescents are looking toward the future, wondering what they are going to do with their lives, and starting to make plans for their careers. Late adolescents are able to gather several pieces of information and make logical judgments based on that information. In those days, it was normal to get married at the age of eighteen or nineteen. In other words, about a century ago, young women had to deal with their sexuality for only two or three years before they got married. They also were at a stage of cognitive development where they were well able to make critical sexual decisions.

Today, young girls often experience their first sexual feelings when they are in the stage of development called early adolescence. In this early phase of development, they are not yet able to make decisions based on their ability to reason. They often have a difficult time putting several pieces of information together and coming up with a logical decision based on that information. They more commonly make their decisions based on the influence of others. Soon after their first period, girls enter the phase of middle adolescence characterized by risk taking behaviors. In this phase of development they have little concept of cause and effect. They do not understand that a certain behavior may lead to some specific consequence. So, today, young women get married around their twenty-fourth or twenty-fifth birthday after struggling with their sexual urges for more than a decade, struggling with these urges during the periods of development when they aren't yet necessarily thinking about consequences or the future. So yes, regarding sexuality, things have really changed over the past few centuries.

Only a decade or two ago, parents and other adults talked about *preventing* premarital sex. Most current talk is about *delaying* sexual activity, having given up on the idea that preventing sex until marriage is even possible. Many adults believe that because sex desires are natural, that young people should be allowed to explore their sexuality and the role of the adult is simply to guide them through this process. This is dangerous ground!

"The risks of acquiring a sexually transmitted disease (STD) is one of the most significant and immediate risks to the health and well-being of adolescents," state well-known researchers (D'Angelo & DiClemente, 1996). STD's impose very substantial economic tolls on health-care systems and cause health problems in young people.

The increase in both the number of STDs and the rates of these infections in young people are directly related to the decrease in the age of sexual initiation by teenagers. The average age of first intercourse is less than sixteen years and much lower in some specific groups. Women who initiate intercourse by the age of fifteen are four times more likely to have ten or more lifetime sexual partners than women who initiate intercourse by the age of twenty years (D'Angelo & DiClemente, 1996).

Young women are biologically vulnerable to becoming infected with an STD. For up to three to four years following the first menstrual period, a very thin layer of cells covers the female cervix. Because of this, young women are more susceptible to becoming infected with an STD when they become sexually active at a young age. This thin, relatively non-protective membrane that covers the cervix will mature and become more protective. Based on biology alone, young girls are more susceptible to sexually transmitted infections.

So, what can be done? If sex-education classes at school aren't sufficient, what is?

Recent research gives us great hope. It has to do with communication. We are aware that there may be fear within some that communication regarding sex increases the odds of a child engaging in sex, but this notion has not been confirmed by research.

One study examined approximately 10,000 students in grades 7 to 11. These young people were interviewed and asked how they felt their parents viewed birth control and their own sexual practices. The finding revealed that if the parents were supportive of the use of birth control and that if the parents had communicated this to their children, the kids were more likely to use birth control. The authors also reported that when there was a high level of satisfaction between the young person and their mother, that there was a lower probability of both sexual intercourse and pregnancy (Jaccard & Dittus, 2000). While these studies include the use of birth control, we are not advocating its use. We are focused on preventing early sexual intercourse.

Would you rather: (a) wait until your youngster is engaged in sex to discuss the need for birth control or (b) work on developing a relationship with your kids that they perceive as highly satisfying, which would result in an decreased probability that they would engage in sex?

Another study examined communication about sexual issues with mothers, fathers, and friends. The researchers report that both male and female adolescents are more likely to discuss sex-based topics with their mothers than with their fathers. Adolescents in this study who reported discussing a number of sex-related topics with their mothers were less likely to have initiated sexual intercourse and more likely to have conservative values about sex. Both males and females were more likely to have discussed sexual intercourse with friends than with parents (DiIorio & Hockenberry-Eaton, 1999).

Although a few studies have shown that parental communication regarding sex is associated with lower rates of sexual intercourse among young people, some large-scale studies have not confirmed that direct communication had this benefit (Newcomer & Udry, 1985; Weeks et al., 1997); But don't give up. This doesn't mean that you shouldn't communicate, it means that we may have to look further than communication *alone* as a prevention strategy. How about communication plus something else?

DiBlasio & Benda (1990) report that sexually active adolescents are less likely than non-sexually active adolescents to report a feeling of closeness to their parents while at the same time believing that their parents would be upset to learn that their child was sexually active. Other researchers report that sexual activity and lack of contraception use among girls age 9 to 15 are related to the girls' belief that their mothers would not care if they became pregnant (Stanton et al., 1994). Do your kids think that you don't care if they are sexually active? Do you really know if they truly understand your feelings about this very serious issue?

One fairly consistent and encouraging finding in research examining associations between parent-child communication and adolescent sexual behavior is this: young people tend to have a later onset of sexual intercourse, fewer number of sexual partners, and more consistent use of contraceptives when they reported a generally good pattern of communication with their parents (O'Sullivan et al., 1999). When parents are perceived as having friendly, attentive styles of communication, their adolescents report less sexual activity in junior high school, high school, and college. Conversely, when adolescents perceive their parents as contentious, dramatic, and dominant, they reported more sexual activity (Mueller & Powers, 1990).

Communication matters. But notice that communication along with a friendly or caring style is even better and may be more effective in preventing or delaying sex among your youngsters.

First develop a relationship of love, and then in the context of that relationship, open the doors of communication. Tell young people about your values. Let them know how you feel about sex. After you do this, think about what you told them, or evaluate your message. Spend some time examining whether or not you told them exactly what you wanted to and then at a later date, not too much later, tell them again. Then re-evaluate. Keep working at refining your message. Once you have it nailed down, repeat it often enough that you are absolutely certain that you have been understood.

You may want to consider asking your kids to tell you what they heard you say when you talked to them about sex or any important issue such as drugs, alcohol, etc. They may tell you something much different from what you think you told them. Communication is very interesting. What you say and what is heard may be two very different things.

We are reminded of a story of a woman, Ann, of about 40 years of age, who took her six-year-old daughter into a physician's office for an emergency visit. The mother told how she had caught her husband of fifteen years sexually molesting the youngster. The doctor immediately called the police and the father was arrested. Needless to say, the mother was distraught. She wondered how such a thing could have ever happened in her home.

Her husband had been married several times during his 20s and early 30s and fathered fourteen other children, eight of them daughters.

Over the ensuing several weeks, Ann contacted each of eight other daughters to explain what had happened. She was alarmed to learn that her husband had molested each and every one of them. The oldest one was twenty years of age and cried as she told of the repeated incestuous attacks from her father.

Ann asked, "Why didn't you tell me?" Through the sobs came a chilling reply, "I did." Ann had been told but didn't hear.

Do you hear your kids when they talk? If they say something very sensitive that alarms you, are you willing to re-gather yourself and forge into scary territory with them?

The need for clear communication cannot be overemphasized. Are you saying what you want to say? Are your kids hearing what you think you said? The only way to find out is to ask them. Be willing to test your communication skills with your kids.

So why all of this talk about sex in a book written for a Christian audience? Maybe you are thinking that we are talking about someone other than your own kids.

A colleague of ours was invited recently to talk to a parent-teacher association at a Christian school. The topic was teen pregnancy. Early in his presentation, he got the sense that the audience was not terribly interested in the subject. He stopped and asked the question, "How many of you have kids who are having sex?" No hands were raised. He then asked a second question, "How many of your kids have friends who are sexually active?" All of the hands in the audience went up. Do you get it? Is your head in the sand regarding your own children and their behaviors?

Even students who attend Christian churches and Christian schools can become sexually experienced at a young age. A study that we conducted regarding sex and drugs among students attending Seventh-day Adventist (SDA) high schools revealed that 16% were sexually experienced (Hopkins, Hopp et al., 1998). Two other studies done in SDA high schools reported that approximately one quarter of their samples were sexually experienced (Ludescher, 1992; Benson & Donahue, 1990). A study conducted among 3,103 Mormon high-school-aged youth reported that 10% of males and 17% of females reported having had sexual intercourse. Some female students reported that the strongest temptations they faced were "boys and sex" (Top & Chadwick, 1998).

Youth associated with religious organizations are not exempt from the pressures to have sex. This is a problem we all must face. Putting our heads in the sand is dangerous; it keeps us from focusing on what can be done. And, as we have seen, there are things that can be done that have the potential to be effective. Relationships that open doors of communication are central to preventing or delaying sex among youth.

Let's say that you are convinced that communication and sound caring relationships with your kids are important. So you start on your plan on strengthening these in your family. Your responsibility is greater that you might suspect.

Many young people live in homes where parents don't take the time to develop strong relationships or communicate. A very large number of kids have only one parent in the home who is so busy providing for the family that the kids are left unattended, often during the afternoon after school hours. This is frightening. Most adolescent girls who become pregnant do so during the after school hours of 3:00 and 6:00 P.M. (Vernon, 1991). This suggests that your responsibility is greater than to your children alone. You must get involved in the lives of other youth.

If you accept the responsibility of including other young people in your life, you will get the opportunity to communicate your values about sex. But first, it is absolutely essential that you start with a caring relationship. You have to first get to know them and let a relationship begin

If you decide to talk to kids about sex without first forming a caring relationship, you may be seen as a sexual predator. Start by learning their names; then take time to talk and nurture relationships. Over time, you will have the opportunity to share your values about sex in a very appropriate manner. Please don't stop a youngster in the hallway at church and say, "Hey kid, I want to talk to you about sex." That can be seriously misunderstood.

It all starts with relationships that, as you recall, are central to the development of a positive self-esteem and the fostering of resilience among youth.

Sexual intercourse among young people is happening very early in their lives. You can probably change this. Your dedication to developing relationships with young people starting at a very early age will open the doors of communication, a valuable tool in preventing or delaying sex among our youth.

Matt isn't sexually experienced. He has three key individuals in his life—his mom, Miss Rae, and Uncle Vanny—who have taken the opportunity to develop special relationships with him and who at appropriate times have communicated to him their feelings regarding sex.

Remember, actively helping young people with the issue of sex is not communication alone but rather relationships plus communication.

Benson, P. L., and M. J. Donahue. 1990. *Valuegenesis: Report I. A Study of the Influence of Family, Church, and School on the Faith, Values and Commitment of Adventist Youth.* Minneapolis: Search Institute.

D'Angelo, L. J., and R. J. DiClemente. 1996. "Sexually Transmitted Diseases Including Human Immunodeficiency Virus Infection." In, *Handbook of Adolescent Health Risk Behavor,* Eds. R. J. DiClemente, W. B. Hansen, & L. E. Ponton. New York: Plenum Press.

DiBlasio, F. A., and B. B. Benda. 1990. "Adolescent Sexual Behavior: Multivariate Analysis of a Social Learning Model." *Journal of Adolescent Research,* 5: 449–466.

DiIorio, C., and M. Hockenberry-Eaton. 2000. "Communication About Sexual Issues: Mothers, Fathers and Friends." *Journal of Adolescent Health, 24*(3): 181–189.

Hopkins, G. L., J. Hopp, H. Hopp Marshak, C. Neish, and G. Rhoads. 1998. "AIDS Risk Among Students Attending Seventh-day Adventist Schools in North America." *Journal of School Health, 68*(4): 141–145.

Jaccard, J., and P. J. Dittus. 2000. "Adolescent Perceptions of Material Approval of Birth Control and Sexual Risk Behavior." *American Journal of Public Health, 90*(9): 1426–1430.

Kreipe, R. E., and O. J. Z. Sahler. 1991. "Physical Growth and Development in Normal Adolescents." In *The Health of Adolescents,* Ed. W. R. Hendee, 21-57. San Francisco: Jossey–Bass.

Ludescher, G. 1992. *AIDS-related knowledge, Attitudes and Behaviors in Adolescents Attending Seventh-day Adventist Schools in California.* Unpublished doctoral dissertation, Loma Linda University, Loma Linda, California.

Mueller, K. E., and W. G. Powers. 1990. "Parent-Child Sexual Discussion: Perceived Communicator Style and Subsequent Behavior." *Adolescence, 25*: 469–482.

Newcomer, S. F., and J. R. Udry. 1985. "Parent-Child Communication and Adolescent Sexual Behavior." *Family Planning Perspectives, 17*: 169–174.

O'Sullivan, L. F., B. M. S. Jaramillo, D. Moreau, and H. F. L. Meyer-Bahlburg. 1999. "Mother-Daughter Communication About Sexuality in a Clinical Sample of Hispanic Adolescent Girls." *Hispanic Journal of Behavioral Sciences, 21*(4): 447–469.

Stanton, B., X. Li, M. Black, I. Ricardo, J. Galbraith, L. Kaljee, and S. Feigelman. 1994. "Sexual Practices and Intentions Among Preadolescent and Early Adolescent Low-income Urban African-Americans." *Pediatrics, 93*: 966–973.

Top, B. L., and B. A. Chadwick. 1998. "Raising Righteous Children"*Brigham Young Magazine, 52*(2): 40–51.

Vernon, M. E. L. 1991. "Life-Style, Risk Taking, and Out-of-Control Behavior." Pp. 162-185 in *The Health of Adolescents,* Ed. W. R. Hendee. San Francisco: Jossey-Bass.

Weeks, K., S. R. Levy, A. K. Gordon, A. Handler, C. Perhats, and B. R. Flay. 1997. "Does Parental Involvement Make a Difference? The Impact of Parent Interactive Activities on Students in a School-based AIDS Prevention Program." *AIDS Education and Prevention, 9*: 90–106.

School as a Community

Matt's high school is pretty much like one in your community. He takes classes from several different teachers in any given day. At the end of a semester, he often moves out of one class and into another with a new instructor, although some of his courses last an entire year. In any given year Matt interacts with ten or twelve different teachers on a daily basis. This is typical for a student in the second year of high school.

Matt's teachers usually have twenty-five to thirty students in their classes. Most are well trained and capable of performing their professional duties well. If you had the opportunity to sit down with any or all of them, you would learn that most teachers wish that they had more time to develop personal relationships with their students, including Matt. Their work duties, however, are so demanding that there is not enough time to make this happen. So, we have students needing meaningful relationships with adults, teachers who are in an optimal position to be those persons, who are so busy that they can only bond with a handful of students each year. Many parents would argue that their situation is similar to that of teachers: not enough time to spend with their kids.

The concept of "school as a community" has made for interesting research. Roberts and colleagues (1995) examined to what extent students in grade school sensed that their school was a functional community. In their work, they defined "school as a community" as a place where students and teachers care about and support each other, actively participate in activities and decisions relating to school, feel a sense of belonging and identification within the school group, and have common goals and values (Roberts et al., 1995). The questions used in this study included how much "my class is like a family," "I feel like I can talk to teachers in this school about things that are bothering me," and "in my class the teacher asks the students to help decide what the class should do," and others.

The idea was to explore to what extent the students and the teachers sensed that their school was like a family or a caring community. Some of the interesting findings were that students' sense of community is not significantly related to school size but that the teachers' sense of community is associated with the school size. They found that as students get older, they are less likely to sense school as a community.

One question you might ask is, "So what if students perceive school as a community or not? They are there to learn." Listen up.

When students had a high perception of their school as a community, they tended to read more outside of school, enjoy reading more, enjoy class more, like school more, avoid work less, and were more academically motivated. They trusted and respected school more, enjoyed helping others learn more, had higher educational aspirations and higher educational expectations. Academically, they performed higher on reading and math achievement tests. In the area of personal attitudes and behaviors, they had more concern for others, higher self-esteem, and resolved conflicts better.

When teachers had a high perception of their school as a community they had higher expectations for student learning, trusted students more, enjoyed teaching more, were more satisfied with teaching, and had a higher overall satisfaction with their job. When the school climate was rated as having a high sense of community, the principal was more competent and supportive, parents were more supportive, and there were more positive teacher-student relations.

Stop here. Go back and read the last two paragraphs again. Do you want your local school to be stellar? Get involved in planning how to make it a place where students and teachers view their school as having is a high "sense of community"! Make it a place where people are cared for, where relationships are encouraged and nurtured, where parents get involved rather than criticize.

Two of the researchers involved in the previously mentioned study went on to examine whether a high sense of community in school was associated with problem behaviors among students (Battistich & Hom, 1997). They found that when students have a high perception of school as a community, the kids were involved with less disruptive behavior and less drug use. *Again, less disruptive behavior and less drug use.*

Getting involved with young people and helping to create school as a community even has an added benefit of fostering a moral character in young people. Battistich (1998) in a presentation at Fresno State University stated that:

> . . . a commitment to care is the basis for morality, and children learn to become caring by being in caring relationships. The research literature provides considerable support for this thesis. Children who grow up to be characterized as "morally mature" have parents who are warm, trusting, and responsive to their needs. Similarly, a few studies have been conducted found that students of teachers who are considered warm and supportive are more helpful and cooperative than those teachers who are either more "businesslike" and task-oriented, or who are harsh and punitive.
>
> The importance of positive interpersonal relationships to moral socialization is hardly surprising. As social beings, we have a need to belong to a group, to feel accepted and valued by others. We seek relationships with those who meet this need, and strive to maintain these relationships by complying with the wishes of those who care for us, adopting their beliefs and values, and imitating their behavior. Although their relative importance varies over the course of development, this applies both to relationships with significant adults, such a parents, teachers, and to relationships with peers. Thus, a school environment which is characterized by caring and supportive relationships between teachers and students and among students should be optimal for promoting prosocial and moral development, in that such an environment is one which both provides

abundant models of behavior consistent with prosocial and moral attitudes and values, and motivates the student to adopt and internalize these attitudes, values and behaviors.

Another study conducted by researchers at the University of Minnesota examined students perception of "connectedness" and its relationship to problem behaviors among young people. Connectedness is very similar to "sense of community" as previously described. The questions examined were to what extent young people felt connected to a parent or parents and also their connectedness at school. The findings, again, are powerful:

Regardless of the number of parents in the household, whether families were rich or poor, regardless of race and ethnicity, children who reported feeling connected to a parent are protected against many different kinds of risks including emotional distress, suicidal thoughts and attempts; cigarette, alcohol, and marijuana use; violent behavior, and early sexual activity (Resnick, 1997).

When these same students felt a high sense of connectedness at school, they were involved in fewer violent acts, were protected from cigarettes, alcohol, and marijuana use, delayed first sexual intercourse, and overall, school connectedness was consistently associated with better health and healthier behaviors among students (Resnick, 1997).

All of these benefits occurred because there were people who were willing to develop relationships with students and create a caring environment. Does that sound like Christian love?

Over the past few years we have seen violence explode in the form of school shootings. Students have been murdered, communities terrorized, and parents left feeling helpless. These are always horrible events. Then we watch as politicians react with their suggested solutions. These might include tighter gun control, teaching students about "choices," installing metal detectors, placing full-time, armed police on campuses, classes on violence, getting rid of violent video games, prohibiting movie violence, and so on. You've heard it. You have agreed or disagreed with some of it. After a few short weeks, the dust settles, and the attention to school violence fades into the background.

So, what can be done? Realistically, is there anything promising that can be done to protect our kids from harm?

As mentioned previously, when students perceive school as a community, they are less involved in disruptive behavior. Students who feel connected at school commit fewer violent acts. Recent research adds other ideas that can lead us to assist in preventing school violence.

One important study reported the value in students' "bonding" at school. How do you encourage bonding? They found that schools that promote prosocial, cooperative behavior, and a culture of learning are central to preventing violence (Hawkins et al., 1998). We do that by providing assistance to schools with people who care, people who are willing to develop relationships with students. We do it by creating an environment of caring people.

A report from the U.S. Department of Health and Human Services (1998) reported that youth are protected from violence when they:

- Have good relationships with their parents
- Have parents who are more frequently present in the home at key times of the day
- Feel connected at school
- Are good students
- Are treated fairly by teachers
- Do not perceive that other students are prejudiced
- Have mentors (who provide career role-modeling)
- Are involved in after-school activities

Mentoring has received much attention recently. A mentor is someone who is willing to develop a relationship and be a resource to another person. This certainly applies to youth and preventing dangerous behaviors. Some measurable values in mentoring have been demonstrated in several different studies.

The United States Department of Justice reports research that was conducted to identify the value in mentoring relationships (Big Brothers and Sisters of America, 1992). Their findings demonstrated that mentored youth are:

- 46% less likely to initiate drug use (70% less likely if they were of a minority race)

- 27% less likely to initiate alcohol use
- 53% less likely to skip school
- 37% less likely to skip class
- Greater than 30% less likely to hit someone
- More confident in their school work
- Got along better with their family

The California Mentor Foundation (2000) reports that of 57,000 mentored youth:
- 98.4% stayed in school
- 85.25% did not use drugs
- 97.9% did not become a teen parent
- 98.2% did not join a gang

Young people need strong enduring relationships with adults. Synthesis of the research suggests that caring adults can play a strong and critical role in protecting students not only from involvement in violent acts, but may have far-reaching benefits even in the area of substance abuse and early sexual activity (Hopkins, 2000).

Let's refocus and examine Christian education. On the surface, one might think that Christian schools are places where students will experience a high sense of community resulting in all of the benefits mentioned previously. After all, the term "Christian education" implies an environment of caring and love, one of cooperation and celebration of Christian beliefs. Do students who attend Christian schools actually perceive a high sense of community? Well, perhaps.

Christian schools face special challenges. When these schools are supported by constituent churches, interesting things can happen. Members of these constituencies may take ownership to the extent that individual church members feel free to place special demands on the school. These demands can cause a slow erosion of the mission of the school to create a Christlike environment. We are aware of parents who complain that their students should be allowed to dress any way that they want to, in spite of school regulations and standards. In the case of small schools where budgets are tight, the loss of a single student's tuition can create budget problems. One way of keeping the student and his or her tuition is to give in to the parents' demands and overlook the dress codes.

Constituent church members may feel free to criticize teachers for allowing students to listen to secular music or attend movies. Other members don't feel that either of these behaviors are worth worrying about. Tensions commonly build, and teachers may find it necessary to switch their church membership to non-constituent churches in order to avoid unfriendly comments or rejection on their day of worship. Some teachers may resign and move on to public education where school policy is dictated by an elected school board rather than a board appointed by constituent churches.

All of this behavior is counterproductive to what we know schools need in order to provide the best in Christian education. Rather than disagreeing with school and complaining, it would be much wiser to get involved by spending two or three hours each week at school and to be a part of the process necessary to create an environment where students perceive their school to be a functional community.

All of the criticism that commonly occurs between churches and their schools is exactly what schools don't need. What they need is to be able to go to church to mobilize members to get involved. People may feel less inclined to volunteer at school when they hear a constant stream of criticism. Getting volunteers to assist at school and mentor students is a gigantic chore on its own without all of the disturbing complaints.

When you decide to take the findings of the research presented in this chapter and start a process of finding people to come to school to help create a community and sense of connectedness, don't overlook the retired members of your church and local faith community. This group could be central to success in creating an effective community in your school.

One more question: To what extent is your church a place where young people feel connected or sense church to be a functional community? Do you find that the young people in your church get up in the morning anxious and happy to be greeted and smiled at when they enter the sanctuary? If not, you've got a problem. It is imperative that church be a place where youngsters feel welcome and cared for. The young people are the future of your church. They are more important than you are to the success of your church.

Matt, your kids, and all of the kids in your town deserve to attend schools and churches where adults are committed to be involved and to create an environment critical to the success and protection of youth from drugs, sex, and violence.

Battistich, V. 1998. "The Effects of Classroom and School Practices on Students' Character Development." Presented at the Character Education Assessment Forum, Bonner Center for Character Education and Citizenship, California State University, Fresno, California. http://www.devstu.org

Battistich, V., and A. Hom. 1997. "The Relationship Between Students' Sense of their School as Community and Their Involvement in Problem Behaviors." *American Journal of Public Health, 87*(12): 1997–2001.

Big Brothers and Sisters of America. www.bbbsa.org

California Mentor Foundation 2000. www.calmentor.com/html/body_about.html

Hawkins, J. D., D. P. Farrington, and R. F. Catalano. 1998. "Reducing Violence Through the Schools." In *Violence in American Schools,* Eds. D. S. Elliott, B. A. Hamburg, and K. R. Williams, 188–216. New York: Cambridge Press.

Hopkins, G. L. 2000. "The Role of the Community in Preventing School Violence." Pp. 2:48-2:49 in, *Stop the Violence: Resource Guide to Safe Schools,* Eds. J. Gulledge and S. Beard. Aspen Publishers: Maryland.

Mann, R., I. Borowsky, A. Stolz, E. Latts, C. U. Cart, and C. D. Brindis. 1998. *Youth Violence: Lessons Learned From the Experts.* Division of General Pediatrics and Adolescent Health, Department of Pediatrics, University of Minnesota and the Division of Adolescent Medicine, Department of Pediatrics and Institute for Health Policy Studies, School of Medicine, University of California.

Resnick, M. D., P. S. Bearman, R. W. Blum, K. E. Bauman, K. M. Harris, J. Jones, J. Tabor, T. Beuhring, R. E. Sieving, M. Shew, M. Ireland, L. H. Bearinger, J. Udry. 1997. "Protecting Adolescents From Harm: Findings From the National Longitudinal Study on Adolescent Health." *Journal of the American Medical Association, 278*(10): 823–832.

Roberts, W., A. Hom, and V. Battistich. 1995. "Assessing Students' and Teachers' Sense of the School as a Caring Community" (paper presented at the American Educational Research Association, April 1995).

Drinking, Drugs, and You

Matt could hardly wait to tell his mom the exciting news. A local computer store, a member of a national chain, had opened up three afternoon jobs for qualified high-school students. They wanted sales people who were young to interact with other young customers in the computer and software departments. This news was of particular interest to Matt as he was sort of a computer wizard. Since his grandfather gave him a new computer for Christmas a couple of years before, Matt seemingly learned all there was to know about computers. He could easily add new software programs or remove others when he no longer needed them.

Matt had learned how to take the computer apart, and he recently added a new CD Rom drive, memory, and even a hard drive. None of this seemed difficult for him. He just sort of had a knack for it. He really loved working on his computer, and he liked going to the computer store and looking at new models and accessories, and he liked walking around the seemingly endless racks of software and finding new programs and games. Matt loved the games, too; he had conquered most of the popular ones.

The news from the local computer store came as sort of a surprise as he had heard that you had to be eighteen years old in order to get a job. Matt later learned that these new openings were an experimental program sponsored by his state for kids younger than eighteen who showed a promise for entering the field of computer science.

What a break! Matt was waiting for his mom when she got home from work to share the great news. She listened with interest as she had often tried to find creative ways of engaging Matt's after-school hours. He made her promise that she would drop by the store during her lunch hour to get more details and pick up application material.

So the next day, she visited the personnel department and got all of the details and forms. It sounded like Matt had a great chance.

That evening Matt waited for his mom to get home so that he could drill her for the details. It seemed simple. The store wanted a few students just like him. All he had to do was to fill out the employment application form, take it to the store after school, and be interviewed by the personnel director. If he passed the interview, the only thing left to do was to have a urine drug screen; when this was found to be negative, he would start work the next Monday. He listened intently, took the application form, and disappeared into his room.

When Matt didn't come out of his room for some hours, his mom went to his room to see how he was doing. She figured that he was probably having a problem completing the long form. When she opened the door, she found Matt sitting at his desk gazing out the window. He seemed to have lost his fire.

She asked if she could help and he declined, saying that he would get to the application after he had more time to think. That didn't seem like him, but his mom didn't think too much about it and went back to what she was doing. After another hour or so she went back and found that Matt was still gazing out the same window. She knew something was wrong. "What's the matter, Matt? Something is bothering you."

He cautiously asked her if she knew how long marijuana stayed in a person's system after using it. She told him that she didn't know. Then it clicked. "Do we need to talk?"

Matt's head didn't turn, but his eyes moved to hers and he said, "I can't apply for the job." He looked sad, very distant, and depressed.

Matt told how he and a couple of friends had smoked marijuana on five or six occasions during the past couple of months. It wasn't something that he had ever wanted to do, but it just sort of happened. One day, an older student had picked Matt and a friend up after school and while cruising around town, the driver pulled out some pot and said, "Want some?" Matt tried it. It seemed to affect him hardly at all except that he felt a little tired. His buddy explained that you have to use it a few times before you feel the real "high."

He thought about what he had done. It didn't seem so bad, and he tried it again a couple of times and sure enough, he felt a little goofy. It was a sort of calm, a different kind of feeling. He didn't seem out of control. He also felt a little guilty as he thought his mom was terrific, and he knew he would really let her down if she ever found out. Matt's thoughts had nothing to do with a fear of becoming hooked but more to do with disappointing his mother. She had spoken to him about using drugs during their evening chats, so he knew how she felt. He was sure she would be crushed if she ever found out. He even wondered if she would reject him, although he doubted it.

As he told his story, his mom simply listened. She had no clue what to do but to listen. So that's what she did. She listened. At the end of Matt's description of his experience with marijuana, his mom simply said, "I guess you are lucky, Matt. Some people start using drugs and don't realize the consequences until they are addicted, flunk out of school, or are put in jail." Matt knew what she meant. His consequences lay right in front of him. He couldn't apply for the job of his immediate dreams, as he couldn't afford to take a drug test that would certainly be positive for the presence of marijuana. Drugs had already gotten in the way of something he really wanted: a job working with computers.

Matt's mom hugged him and assured him that although she didn't understand why people used drugs and even though he had experimented a few times, she still loved him. She didn't love him based upon his use or non-use of marijuana; she loved him in spite of it. His use of marijuana *did* matter to her; she didn't want him to use again. But in her eyes, he was still terrific; he was a treasure; there was nothing that he could do to keep her from loving him.

"You mean you aren't mad at me," he asked? She explained that there was nothing in her heart that even came close to anger; she was worried for him and the possibility there could be more drug use in his future.

From that day on, Matt's mom paid more attention to how he spent his time. Before this event with the marijuana, she really hadn't worried about him, and though she was sure that many kids at school were using drugs, he just seemed normal and had never shown any signs of what she would expect if he were using drugs. His grades hadn't dropped, he had never seemed intoxicated, he wasn't suddenly missing school. His teachers had not reported any problems. All had seemed well with Matt.

She didn't know what to do except to try to get closer to him. That was tough to figure out how to do as they were already very close. One afternoon at work, with the radio going in the background, she heard a drug expert being interviewed. She didn't hear the whole report but did pick up on one phrase. "Before it happens, rehearse with your kids what they will say or do when faced with drugs or sex." Matt's mom thought to herself, "Matt always knew how I felt about drugs, but I didn't ever rehearse anything with him." She decided to give it a try.

Matt was heading out to an evening basketball game at his high school. His mom drove him. During the ride they chatted and she asked him, "Hey, Matt, if someone offers you some marijuana again, what are you going to do or say?"

He told her that he was going to refuse it. She pressed on, "No, tell me exactly what you will say." He didn't know.

She suggested, "I don't know exactly what you should say but consider this. Tell them 'No thanks.' Just try that." He thought about it and didn't say much. She didn't pursue the issue any further.

Matt wasn't offered marijuana that evening, but a couple of weeks later a friend with whom he had used marijuana in the past offered him some. Matt said, "No thanks. I don't think I want to do that any more." It was that simple. His friend sort of shrugged his shoulders and went on with what he was doing.

That evening Matt told his mom what had happened, and with a grin he said, "And it felt pretty good to have something to say." Matt was obviously proud of having made a good decision and very proud that he had pleased his mother.

Not too many days later, Matt's mom asked him if he had ever tried alcohol. He said, "Well, a few times." She seemed puzzled and asked him if he felt awkward about talking about it. He said, "No. I'm not afraid to talk to you about anything. Since the marijuana thing, I realized that I am pretty much OK coming to you for any reason."

The conversation continued, and she asked him what type of alcohol he had used and he said, "Beer a few times and then wine once. The wine was horrible. It was warm and tasted like spoiled grapes."

"Where did you get the beer and wine?" she asked.

His answer shocked her. "At home, Mom. You keep it around the house. I tried it a few times after school when you were at work. When you talked to me about drinking, I thought you meant with my friends."

Matt's mom wasn't a big drinker but she did keep beer and wine on hand for times when friends would drop by to visit. He had never seen her drunk or any signs of alcohol abuse.

After this incident, Matt's mom removed all forms of alcohol from the home for good. She no longer used any alcohol either in the home or socially. It just wasn't worth the risk. She needed to do a better job of modeling proper behavior for Matt and his little sister.

It is interesting how much we talk to young people regarding the hazards of drugs, yet many use alcohol in our homes. We commonly hear that kids need to be taught to drink responsibly. Well, why teach them to drink at all? There are well-known hazards associated with alcohol use. This information isn't new.

In research that we did several years ago on students attending Seventh-day Adventist high schools, we asked 1,748 students—of whom 93.3% were Seventh-day Adventists—if they had a parent who currently used alcohol, tobacco, or marijuana. We found that the substance most commonly used by a parent was alcohol (25.7%), followed by tobacco (10.7%), and lastly marijuana (4.5%). These students and their parents were Seventh-day Adventists, who as a religion do not believe in the use of any of these three substances. These substances are being used even in this very conservative religion.

We then questioned students regarding their personal use of several substances and compared their use of several different drugs based upon whether or not they had a parent who used alcohol, tobacco, or marijuana. We found that when the parents used at least one of these three substances, there was a much greater risk that their students were using all drugs measured (Hopkins, Hopp et al., 1998). The home is no place for alcohol or any other drug.

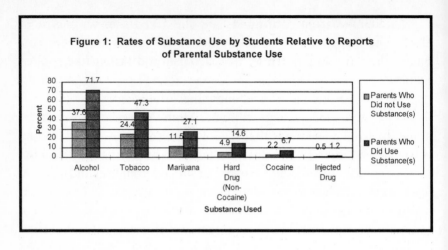

Figure 1: Rates of Substance Use by Students Relative to Reports of Parental Substance Use

Further, we investigated whether the use of substances by the students and by the parents might be associated with the students' sexual experience. We found that students who used or had tried drugs were more sexually experienced than those who had not. We also found that students were more likely to be sexually experienced if they had a parent who used alcohol, tobacco, or marijuana (Hopkins, Hopp et al., 1998). The findings of this research are powerful. Among the students who had never tried a drug and whose parents were not using any drugs, only 3.5% of the students were sexually experienced. When both the student and parent(s) used any substance, the students' rate of sexual experience increased tenfold. Substance use and sex among kids are intimately related.

Substance Use		Sexually Experienced Students
Parent	Student	Percentage
No	No	3.5%
Yes	No	5.9%
No	Yes	26.3%
Yes	Yes	30.3%

A large study of Mormon high school students revealed that 20% of those in the twelfth grade had used tobacco and 20% had tried alcohol (Top & Chadwick, 1998).

We have to come to terms with the fact that even in the most conservative religious environments, our young people are using drugs at some level. All of the kids who try tobacco, alcohol, or any other drug will not necessarily go on to become addicts. But problem behaviors associated with drug use—and of course addictions—can start with a single use.

When our kids do experiment with substances or sex, however, we must not give up and reject them. We must get closer to them and find ways of assisting them in making better decisions in the future. Never give up! The late Carroll O'Connor, a TV actor, made a powerful television commercial after his son became addicted to drugs and ultimately committed suicide. O'Connor begged the television audience, "Put yourself between your kids and drugs. Do whatever it takes." These were powerful words of a grieving father.

Matt's mom played her hand correctly. After the incident with marijuana, she relied upon her love for him and she refined her communication strategies to arm Matt with strategies to better face tough situations. At the time she learned of Matt's drug use, she could have straightened up, screamed, cried, or gone through all sorts of gyrations in an attempt to scare him into nonuse. She chose the correct road.

The screaming and yelling would only have served to drive a wedge between the two of them. Matt would then have been more isolated, alone in trying to figure out how to navigate through future times when he would face tough decisions. This was a time when Matt needed her to get closer, not more distant. As a team they would face the future. Through these incidents with marijuana and alcohol, Matt's mom learned not to expect perfection. She learned rather that she and Matt were a team who would face these challenges together; they would plan together on how to handle tough situations one at a time. Together they would celebrate success and review what had worked. Likewise, as a team they would review decisions that he would make that were not good. Planning, preparing, and loving would be her strategies.

Matt came home from the annual school picnic late one afternoon. His mom asked how the day went. "It was fun. Jenny and I spent the whole day together. I think she is starting to like me, Mom." She smiled.

He continued, "A bunch of the guys brought some beer and asked me if I wanted some. I told them, 'No, I don't think I am going to do that any more.' It worked, Mom. They didn't pressure me. Jenny was excited that I was able to say no." Matt felt good about himself, and he learned that it was OK to say no. It didn't come easy. He was glad that he had something ready to say when the situation presented itself.

After that, Matt's mom talked to him about how he would probably find that even the drug users would respect him for deciding not to "use."

One thing that Matt knew for sure was that handling drug and alcohol decisions wasn't easy. He wondered how he would handle the very powerful urge to engage in sex. That one scared him. He talked to his mom about it, and they went back to the drawing board. They would plan.

Jesus cared for children and illustrated it often in His ministry. Though He was a leader and a powerful teacher, children were not afraid to come to Him. His counsel to all of us is recorded in the gospel of Mark. He took a little child and had him or her stand among them. Taking the child in His arms, He said to the adults crowded around, " 'Whoever welcomes one of these little children in my name welcomes me' " (Mark 9:37, NIV).

Matt's story isn't over yet. He will face tough decisions and situations. He isn't sure whether or not he will be able to postpone sex until marriage. It scares him. But he and his mom continue to talk and plan. Teamwork! It is so much better than leaving him alone to handle difficult situations.

Matt's mom's story isn't complete, either. She isn't sure Matt will always be able to avoid all of the pressures that he will face. She is also very worried about his sexual decisions. One thing is for certain—she will keep the communication stream open. They will plan together all the way through his teen years. She will stay close to him.

She will learn and be able to better plan with her daughter for similar situations.

What about kids whose parents are either absent or so absorbed with their jobs that they just don't take the time to get close to their kids and make plans as Matt's mom has? What about the many young people who have only one parent in the home who is so busy working to provide for the family that applying the strategies we have described just doesn't happen? What about the families where the parents are strict or prone to screaming and yelling?

Very important, what about the parents who threaten eternal damnation and continually use the Bible as a whip to scare their children into conformity? Jesus didn't do this. But so many parents do.

All of these situations should tell us one simple thing. Other kids need us also. All kids need to be loved and cared for. Some won't get love and care at home or even at church where so often no one even knows their names.

As we plan with our children, let's also look around and find other kids to get close to by developing caring relationships. We can let the power of God's love work to bring us to a place where we can carefully make plans with them for the challenges that they will face.

We can't walk up to a young person and sternly say, "I want to talk to you about drugs. Let's plan what you are going to say and do when someone offers you marijuana." That's not where we start. We begin by first learning their names, then getting to know them. We must develop relationships with them. Let God use the power of His love to bring us to the place in a relationship where young people will feel comfortable coming to us with their problems. Or let God bind us with the kids so that we can comfortably talk to them about sensitive issues, things that many kids would fear discussing with their parents. Let's become the "other adults" in the lives of kids around us.

We often hear adults say, "If the teachers just did their jobs, this would have never happened."

Let's face the hard, uncomfortable reality. *The problem is not bad kids, bad teachers, or bad schools. The problem is clearly a lack of adults who care. We are the problem.* Kids need us—and we aren't taking the time to give them what they need. Schools need us to spend two or three hours a week and connect with the kids, thereby creating a sense of community in their school. Relationships with their parent together with relationships with us caring church members are what will ultimately make kids resilient to all of the bad that is going on around them.

Go look in the mirror and face the problem. Then walk away with a plan for how you will learn the names of the young people in your area—especially your church. If you do this well, you will find that when you walk into the local grocery store and see a young person who knows you, they will come to you to at least say "Hi." If they don't, you aren't doing your job well enough. Go to them and greet them with a smile. Eventually they will come to you. Everyone is looking for the warmth of a smile and caring relationship. Everyone.

Plan how you will develop relationships with them. It will change your life. And it may save the life of a young person.

Hopkins, G. L., J. Hopp, H. Hopp Marshak, C. Neish, and G. Rhoads 1998. "AIDS Risk Among Students Attending Seventh-day Adventist Schools in North America." *Journal of School Health, 68*(4): 141–145.

Top, B. L., and B. A.Chadwick. 1998. "Raising Righteous Children." *Brigham Young Magazine, 52*(2): 40–51.

Pornography

One problem that Matt's mom hasn't faced yet is Internet pornography. Matt could be spending time surfing through the many sites on the Internet where there are images of people having sex—graphic images; not just nudity but real sex. She hasn't thought much about it though she has heard about it from time to time.

Though Matt and his mom's relationship is great, is it good enough that he can talk to his mom about pornography if he has a problem with it? Would he be too embarrassed to bring this up? There may be a good chance that he would never go to her to discuss porn. She must confront the reality of this problem, and she must find a way to get the topic on the table.

The reality of Internet pornography is astonishing, and it can start so innocently. Matt's mom read a story about Justin in a magazine one afternoon. Justin was twelve years old and loved to go fishing. His parents lived in a house surrounded by cherry trees. Nearby was a creek with a great fishing hole under a road crossing. One afternoon after school, Justin walked over to his favorite spot next to the crossing and sat down. He sent his baited hook sailing into the perfect spot. As he waited for the tip of his rod to shake, he noticed a brown paper bag sitting a few feet away. This was something new. It hadn't been there a few days before.

He opened the bag, and what he saw sent his heart racing. Suddenly his face felt warm. There, right in front of him was a large full-page picture of a man and a woman having sex—the real thing. As he flipped through the pages, he saw more of the same. His heart beat faster with each new image. Wow! He had never seen anything like this before. He was embarrassed but at the same time very stimulated. All of this seemed terribly interesting, but he knew it wasn't something he could take home with him. After all, what if his mom found it?

Justin didn't even look at his fishing rod to see if a fish might be nibbling. He continued to explore the material.

The next day after school, he went home, grabbed his fishing gear, and headed out to his favorite spot. This time his fingers fumbled as he tried to bait the hook, as he was anxious to spend a few more moments thumbing through the magazine. Justin didn't notice, but he started fishing every day, and on each day, he spent more and more time with his secret. Then, one day the magazine was gone.

Justin was a different boy than on the day he first encountered the magazine. Now he knew what was under the clothes of grown women. Now he knew what sex organs were for, what you did with them, and where they went. He soon began to wonder if he could do the same things he had seen in the magazine. Something in his brain had clicked on; it was like a part of him now was alert that had never been before. He wished that the magazine hadn't disappeared, but he also felt some sense of relief that it wasn't there any more. He was confused yet aroused. All of this was so new to him.

One afternoon while sitting at a computer in the lab at school, he heard a few other students giggle, and then call out, "Justin, come over here. Look at this." He could see from a distance that his classmates had found pictures very similar to the ones he had seen in the magazine at the fishing hole.

"How did you find those pictures?" he asked.

"Don't you know?" They showed him how to find hundreds and hundreds of sexual images within seconds. Nothing to it. Free of charge.

Matt's mom couldn't believe it. A twelve-year-old boy and pornography? Who could believe such a thing?

The next day after work, when Matt was off studying with friends, she asked her daughter, Beth, who was twelve years old, if she had ever seen sex on the Internet.

"Sure," Beth replied.

Mom froze. "How did that happen?"

Beth's story was very similar to the one she had read about. "I was in the computer lab at school looking for pictures of Britney Spears (a popular young pop singer), when suddenly a picture of another person named Britney appeared, only this one wasn't the singer, she was some kind of sex actress. I didn't think too much about it and clicked my mouse to look further for the real Britney Spears when the boys who were standing behind me yelled , 'Go back to those pictures. We want to see what you had on the screen!' "

Beth's mom asked her to go to the computer and show her how it happened. Beth skipped over to the computer, clicked the mouse a couple of times, and waited as the modem connected. Then she looked up at her mom and said, "OK, what do you want me to do?"

With her arms crossed, Beth's mom said, "You told me that you know how to find dirty pictures on the Internet, and since I am from Missouri, show me! I don't believe it."

Beth shrugged her shoulders and said, "Mom, anyone can do it. It's simple." Beth quickly typed a few words on her computer and BINGO! The screen filled with people having sex every way that the mind could imagine. In fact, suddenly one window after another started popping up even though Beth's fingers weren't on the mouse or the keyboard. Automatically, picture after picture appeared.

"Turn it off! I don't want to see that stuff," Mom said. Beth did and swung around in her chair to face her mom. Beth's mom asked if she often went onto the Internet looking for people having sex.

"Mom, I never do it. You asked me to show you, and I did." Beth scolded her mother.

"Well, how did you do it?" asked Mom. Beth started typing again and her mom stopped her. "Just show me how. Don't bring up more pictures. I've seen enough."

Beth explained. "Look, Mom. Just type in the word *sex* and hit the 'enter' key. That will take you to thousands of choices of links that will immediately take you to anything you want to see."

If all of this sounds crazy to you, consider this. An elderly woman lives near the Children's Hospital at Loma Linda University in southern California. She loves to knit and crochet. Over the past two years she has fashioned nearly 300 pairs of booties for the babies at the hospital. One day she wanted to look for more patterns. So she went to her computer and innocently typed in the word *bootee*. Immediately she was presented with a page of over 120,000 different "links" that she could click on to access sexual content. It seems that *bootee* means something much different these days.

It's just that simple. Our kids have access to so many different Web sites that contain sexual content that a person could spend twenty-four hours a day and probably not visit all of them in a year. Online porn is one of the most profitable areas of e-commerce. Estimates of annual revenues range from half a million to billions of dollars. The number of people who visit sex sites each day has been estimated at 60 million. Together, the top five sex sites have more Internet visitors than MSNBC.com and CNN.com combined (Webb, 2001). All of these sites are available to your kids every minute of their lives—to every kid with access to a computer.

Internet porn is so large that it is probably accurate to say that it is here to stay; likely it will never be completely blocked. Every day, approximately 400 new pornographic Web sites open on the Internet from locations such as Thailand and Russia (Hughes, 2001).

In the United States, an estimated 10 million children go online every day. Nearly all of them are anxious to make "e-friends" where they can chat. In a recent study of almost 1,500 children ages 10 to 17 researchers found that one in four had an unwanted exposure to some kind of image of naked people or people performing sexual acts. One in 33 received an aggressive solicitation, meaning that some person on the Internet asked them to meet, phone, or sent them regular mail, money, or gifts (Hughes, 2001).

If you aren't convinced that porn is a problem, keep an eye on your local newspaper. The papers commonly report incidents where individuals such as a dean of a well-known divinity school, a Disney Internet executive, countless college professors, schoolteachers, and other once-reputable citizens are "busted" for viewing Internet porn sites (Jenkins, 2001).

Jenkins (2001) reports:

> Dr. Mark Lasher, a co-founder of the Christian Alliance for
> Sexual Recovery (and himself a recovering "sex addict"), had
> this to say at a Congressional hearing last year: Many in the
> medical community feel that for a substance to be addictive it
> must create a chemical tolerance. Alcoholics know, for example,
> that over the lifetime of their addiction, they must consume
> more and more alcohol to achieve the same effect. New research,
> such as by Drs. Harvey Milkman and Stan Sunderwirth, has
> demonstrated that sexual fantasy and activity, because of natu-
> rally produced brain chemicals, has the ability to create brain
> tolerance to sex. I have treated over a thousand male and female
> addicts. Almost all of them began with pornography.

Jenkins goes on to say:

> The Internet makes porn imagery even more easily avail-
> able, and in virtually limitless variety. It would be a miracle if
> kids weren't finding this stuff, even if it means going around the
> "filters" provided by their parents or their Internet service pro-
> viders. . . . If exposure builds up tolerance, and tolerance makes
> the problem worse, having unlimited porn imagery within easy
> reach of every computer is likely to produce social effects that
> we haven't yet reckoned with.

Matt's mom just had to know if he was accessing Internet porn
sites. She didn't have the courage to ask him directly, although, she had
noted that he spent a lot of time in his room with the door closed while
he surfed the Internet. She hadn't thought about porn until the conversation with Beth.

One afternoon she asked Beth if there was any to know whether
someone has been looking at porn sites on the computer. Beth said,
"Sure. Nothing to it." Beth showed her how to do it.

After learning how to look around on Matt's computer to see what
sites he had been visiting on the Internet, his mom went to his room
one evening when he was gone. She did the things that Beth had taught

her do to, and to her horror, she learned that Matt had visited hundreds of different Internet sex sites.

It took days for her to muster enough courage to talk to him about it, but eventually she did. Matt admitted it. He assured her that it wasn't a problem. She asked him if he would not do it any more, and he assured her that he wouldn't.

The story isn't over for Matt. Whether or not he will visit more porn sites or not is a question that won't be answered until his mother commits to monitoring his Internet activities.

If our description of porn on the Internet seems wild, it isn't. This is serious business, and we must come to terms with it. Leaving children with unsupervised computer access may be as dangerous as expecting them to live inside an adult bookstore without looking around. If your kids have computers with access to the Internet, learn how to supervise their Internet activities. If you don't know how to use a computer, then learn. Ask a friend to show you how to monitor Internet activities. Talk to your kids. Plan what you will do.

A recent article in *Christianity Today* (Gardner, 2001) reported the results of research conducted on their readership, both the laity and clergy, regarding the use of Internet pornography. The author reported that 33% of the clergy and 36% of the laity had visited porn sites. Eighteen percent of the clergy said that they visited sexually explicit sites more than once a week.

In this study, members of the clergy appeared to be more reluctant to tell their spouses about their Internet pornography than did the laity. Twenty percent of calls received on Focus on the Family's Pastoral Care Line are about pastors and online porn (Gardner, 2001).

Pornography is available to everyone. It is treacherous ground. The research on the effects of porn is mixed. You don't have to be a rocket scientist, however, to know that this stuff isn't good for anyone.

Be alert to the fact that porn is available to your kids and other family members. Monitor their computer activities. Try to get this very sensitive topic on the table for discussion. Plan for what you will do if you find it in your home. If there is something that deserves your thoughtful prayer, it is the area of pornography and your young people. Communicate, love unconditionally, and pray for guidance.

Gardner, Christine J. 2001. "Tangled in the Worst of the Web." *Christianity Today*, (March 5): 42–49.

Hughes, J. 2001. "Protecting Kids From Porn." *Christian Science Monitor*, (March 21): 11.

Jenkins, H. W. 2001. "Pornography, Main Street to Wall Street." *Policy Review, 105*(Feb/Mar): 3–11.

Webb, G. 2001. "Sex and the Internet." *Yahoo! Internet Life, 7*(5) (May): 88–97.

Religion, Prayer, and Benefits

The challenges of raising children in a socially toxic social environment has left Matt's mom in a position familiar to all of us. Although many of her parental skills are excellent and have already paid off in Matt's and Beth's lives, she still wonders if she is doing all that she can do. What parent doesn't struggle with similar thoughts and concerns? The issue with pornography has caused her to lose sleep, and she still worries about her kids getting involved with drugs.

She knows that her relationship and communication are essential, but the power of sexual temptation seems larger than any parenting tool she has ever heard of. It is especially so with Internet sex so widely available within seconds on any computer with Internet access. What now? What is so powerful that it could buffer the influence and availability of pornography?

She went to her pastor and asked what more could be done. He suggested prayer. Easy enough. She had always prayed for her kids. But she couldn't help but wonder if there was even more that could be done.

She thought, "What if my church was open minded enough for me to go before them, describe the availability of Internet pornography and drugs, and ask them to intercede in prayer for my kids and for the adults in the church." She couldn't do that. Her kids would be devastated. She couldn't even figure out how to talk about it in church without people walking away knowing that she was talking about either her own problem or that of her kids.

This porn and drug thing is very difficult. You can worry about it, but you can't even talk to others about it without raising suspicion and then suffering the probable brunt of their gossip.

Matt's mom could only imagine the talk behind her back. "Did you hear about Matt and Beth? They are hooked on porn and drugs."

These are difficult problems and very difficult times. What about spirituality and prayer? Is there evidence of the power of these things?

The power of spirituality and prayer have been the focus of considerable research. The findings are amazing. Lampmann (1998) reports the following findings of research in this area:

- Patients are 12 times more likely to survive open-heart surgery if they depend on their religious faith and social support.
- Over a 28-year study period, mortality for frequent attendees of religious services was almost 25% lower than for people who attended less frequently. For women, the figure was 35%.
- Those who attend religious services at least once a week have been shown to have stronger immune-system functioning.
- Greater religious involvement has been associated with lower blood pressure, fewer strokes, lower rates of death from heart disease, lower mortality after surgery, and longer survival in general.
- A strong religious faith and active involvement in a religious community appear to be the combination most consistently associated with better health.
- People who are more religious experience greater well-being and life satisfaction, less depression, less anxiety, and are much less likely to commit suicide.
- Therapies for depression and anxiety that incorporate religious beliefs in treatment result in faster recovery from illness than do traditional therapies.
- Heart-surgery patients who are religious have 20% shorter post-operative hospital stays than nonreligious patients.
- Hospital stays are nearly 2-1/2 times longer for older patients who don't have a religious affiliation.

- Heart-surgery patients assigned chaplain intervention show an average two days shorter length of stay, or about $4,200 cost savings per patient.

Regarding drug use:
- Roman Catholic students who attended church used less marijuana and other drugs (Adlaf and Smart, 1985).
- High-school students who are religious have lower rates of lifetime and previous-month marijuana use (Amoateng et al., 1986).
- Religion, for some youth, effectively reduces the risk of becoming regular users of alcohol and marijuana (Burkett, 1977).
- Narcotic addicts are less involved in religion, are less likely to make decisions to become more interested in religion during adolescence or commit themselves to faith during adulthood (Cancellaro et al., 1982).
- Teen girls who abstain from alcohol are more likely to come from religious homes, to have family rules regarding eating, drinking, and watching television, and to be satisfied with their lives than are girls who are past or current users of alcohol. Positive family environments are critical for young women (Coombs et al., 1985).
- The rates of drug-use behaviors among students attending Seventh-day Adventist high schools are lower than for students who attend public high schools (Hopkins, Hopp et al, 1998a).
- Religious programs are more effective than other programs in establishing abstinence from heroin (Desmond and Maddux, 1981).
- Religious factors, including personal commitment to Christ and belief in God, family values, church teachings, and participation in personal and private religious practices are associated with lower drug use among adolescents in a conservative denomination (Dudley et al, 1987).
- Positive religious attitudes and commitment are related to less alcohol and drug use and to less-permissive attitudes toward these substances among adolescents (Hadaway et al., 1984).
- High religious involvement is associated with lower rates of al-

cohol and drug abuse among patients with mood disorders (Hasin et al., 1985).
- Religion and parental influence are the most common factors associated with abstaining from alcohol (Hughes et al., 1985).
- Alcohol, marijuana, and tobacco among adolescents are related to sexual, delinquent, and social behavior. The use of these three substances is lower with higher academic achievement and religious behavior (Hundleby, 1987).
- Alcoholics are more likely than normal subjects to have a disturbed home environment as children, to reject faith during adolescence, and not to practice religious activities as adults (Larson and Wilson, 1980).
- Lack of religious affiliation is strongly associated with subsequent alcohol abuse among physicians. Students of Jewish affiliation or ancestry are less likely to abuse alcohol (Moore et al., 1990).
- Higher religious commitment among adolescents is associated with lesser intention to use cocaine, which, in turn, is a major determinant in the eventual decision to use cocaine (Newcomb and Bentler, 1986).
- High-school students who attend conservative Protestant religious churches that proscribe alcohol use have lower rates of alcohol use and abuse than other students (Schlegel and Sanborn, 1979).
- Spirituality and religious involvement may be an important protective factor against alcohol/drug abuse (Miller, 1998).
- Religion does provide some protection from drug use by adolescents (Amey et al., 1996).

Regarding sexual behaviors:
- Students who attended the Seventh-day Adventist parochial schools report lower rates of sexual intercourse (16.3% vs. 53.1%) than their counterparts in public schools (Hopkins and Hopp et al., 1998a).
- Measurements designed in accord with the Theory of Planned Behavior reveal that students most relied on spiritual strength and encouragement from a teacher to manage their control over

premarital sexual intercourse (Hopkins and Hopp et al., 1998b).

- More religious attitudes and church attendance of both mothers and their children, along with less permissive attitudes towards adolescent sexuality for both, is associated with reduced levels of sexual activity among adolescents (Thornton and Camburn, 1989).
- Young men and women who are frequent church attendees from conservative religious affiliations and who grow up in a two-parent household are less likely to engage in premarital sex than other Christians (Beck et al., 1991).
- Frequency of church attendance and perception of close friends' permissiveness are significantly related to low levels of sexual permissiveness among black adolescent females (Brown, 1985).
- Maintenance of sexual virginity is associated with increased religiosity and sexual guilt among college students, particularly women (Fox and Young, 1989).
- Higher religious commitment is related to less-permissive sexual views (Haerich, 1992).

There is an abundance of research that demonstrates that religion and spirituality have a potent influence of preventing drug use and sexual behaviors among young people, and our list of research reports only scratches the surface in this area.

There is, however, no specific research directed at prayer or the relationship between church attendance and spirituality on pornography. The Internet is new, and therefore the influences of the dark side of the Internet on our kids are virtually untested in research. You can be assured that researchers are very busy today examining these issues, but the effects may not be known for some years.

In order to moderate the effects of all that is going on in the lives of our kids, it is essential that we develop a strong relationship with God and rely upon His strength. The temptations that our kids face are so powerful that we must rely on the only possible Power in the universe that will protect us and guide us in our relationships. It is absolutely essential that faith communities, that all churches face these problems resolutely. It will take our consecrated effort, guided by the Holy Spirit, to succeed.

Adlif, E. M. and R. G. Smart. 1985. "Drug Use and Religious Affiliation: Feelings and Behavior." *British Journal of Addiction, 80:* 163–171.

Amey, C. H., S. L. Albrecht, and M. K. Miller. 1996. "Racial Differences in Adolescent Drug Use: The Impact of Religion." *Substance Use and Misuse, 31*(10): 1311–1332.

Amoateng, A. Y. and S. J. Bahr. 1986. "Religion and Family Influences on Adolescent Drug Use." *Sociological Perspectives, 29*(1): 53–76.

Beck, S. H., B. S. Cole, and J. A. Hammond. 1991. "Denomination and Premarital Sex Among Young Adults." *Journal for the Scientific Study of Religion, 30*(2): 173–180.

Brown, S. V. 1985. "Permarital Sex Among Black Adolescent Females." *Social Psychology Quarterly, 48*(4): 381–387.

Burkett, S. R. 1977. "Religion, Parental Influence, and Adolescent Alcohol and Marijuana Use." *Journal of Drug Issues, 7*(3): 263-273.

Byrd, R. B. 1988. "Positive Therapeutic Effects of Intercessory Prayer in a Coronary Care Unit Population." *Southern Medical Journal, 81*: 826–829.

Cancellaro, L. A., D. B. Larson, and W. P. Wilson. 1982. "Religious Life of Narcotic Addicts." *Southern Medical Journal, 75*: 1166–1168.

Collipp, P. H. 1969. "The Efficacy of Prayer: A Triple-Blind Study." *Medical Times, 97*: 201–204.

Comstock, G. W., and K. B. Partridge. 1972. "Church Attendance and Health." *Journal of Chronic Diseases, 25*: 665–672.

Coombs, R. H., D. K. Wellisch, and F. Fawzy. 1985. "Drinking Patterns Among Young Women." *American Journal of Drug and Alcohol Abuse, 11*: 315–348.

Desmund, D. P. and J. F Maddux. 1982. "Religious Programs Among Heroin Users." *Journal of Drug and Alcohol Abuse, 8*(1): 71–83.

Dudley, R. L., P. B. Mutch, and R. J. Cruise. 1987. "Religious Factors and Drug Use in Seventh-day Adventist Youth." *Journal for the Scientific Study of Religion, 26*(2): 218–233.

DuRant, R.H., R. Pendergrast, and C. Seymore. 1990. "Sexual Behavior Among Hispanic Female Adolescents." *Pediatrics, 85*(6): 1051–1058.

Fox, E. and M. Young. 1989. "Religiosity, Sex Guilt, and Sexual Behavior in College Students." *Health Values, 13*(2): 32–37.

Hadaway, C. K., K. W. Elifson, and D. M. M. Petersen. 1984. "Religious Commitment and Drug Use in Adolescents." *Journal for the Scientific Study of Religion, 23*(2): 109–128.

Haerich, P. 1992. "Premarital Sexual Permissiveness and Religious Orientation." *Journal for the Scientific Study of Religion 31*(3): 361–365.

Hasin, D., J. Endicott, and Lewis 1985. "Alcohol and Drug Abuse in Patients With Affective Disorders." *Comprehensive Psychiatry23*(6): 283–295.

Hopkins, G. L., J. Hopp, H. Hopp Marshak, C. Neish, and G. Rhoads. 1998. "An AIDS Risk Assessment of Students Attending Christian High Schools in the United States of America: A Practical Application of the Theory of Planned Behavior." *Journal of Research on Christian Education 7*(2) (Autumn): 91–120.

Hopkins, G. L., J. Hopp, H. Hopp Marshak, C. Neish, and G. Rhoads. 1998a. "AIDS Risk Among Students Attending Seventh-day Adventist Schools in North America." *Journal of School Health 68*(4): 141–145.

Hughes, J., M. Stewart, and B. Barraclough. 1985. "Why Teetotalers Abstain." *British Journal of Psychiatry 146*: 204–208.

Hundleby, J. D. 1987. "Adolescent Drug Use in a Behavioral Matrix: A Confirmation and Comparison of Sexes." *Addictive Behaviors 12:* 103–112.

Lampmann, J. 1998. "A Frontier of Medical Research: Prayer." *Christian Science Monitor 90*(82): 4.

Larson, D. B., and W. P. Wilson. 1980. "Religious Life of Alcoholics." *Southern Medical Journal 73*: 723–727.

Miller, W. R. 1999. "Researching the Spiritual Dimensions of Alcohol and Other Drug Problems." *Addiction 93*(7): 979–990.

Moore, R. D., L. Mead, and T. Pearson. 1990. "Youthful Precursors of Alcohol Abuse in Physicians." *American Journal of Medicine 88*: 332–336.

Newcomb, M. D. and P. M. Bentler. 1986. "Cocaine Use Among Adolescents." *Addictive Behaviors 11*: 263–273.

Poloma, M. M. and B. F. Pendleton, 1991. "The Effect of Prayer on Well-being." *Journal of Psychology and Theology 19*: 71–83.

Schlegel, R. P., and M. D. Sanborn. 1979. "Religious Affiliation and Adolescent Drinking." *Journal of Studies on Alcohol 40*(7): 693–703.

Thornton, A., and D. Camburn. 1989. "Religiosity and Sexual Behavior and Attitudes Among Adolescents and Mothers." *Journal of Marriage and Family 51*: 641–653.

Conclusion

Let's make the message of prevention very clear. Our kids need to be loved. In a day when probably most young people brought up in the Christian church will leave their churches about the time that they finish high school, we are faced with a terrible reality. That is, we have probably always had the message of salvation right, but we haven't tested the healing and preventive power of love very well.

The Living Bible says it quite well:

> If I had the gift of being able to speak in other languages without learning them, and could speak in every language there is in all of heaven and earth, but didn't love others, I would only be making noise. If I had the gift of prophecy and knew all about what is going to happen in the future, knew everything about *everything*, but didn't love others, what good would it do? Even if I had the gift of faith so that I could speak to a mountain and make it move, I would still be worth nothing at all without love. If I gave everything I have to poor people, and if I were burned alive for preaching the Gospel but didn't love others, it would be of no value whatever (1 Corinthians 13:1-3).

In the end, when all of the special gifts from God have

come to an end, love will go on. "Three things [will] remain —faith, hope, and love —and the greatest of these is love" (1 Corinthians 13:13).

It is time for love. It is time to get to know every young person, every person by their names. Let the power of love be demonstrated through relationships that begin very simply. Test the power of the Lord, and use His love in helping to prevent the dangerous behaviors that face our young people.

Don't expect special programs to achieve prevention goals. Don't expect excellent preachers, video presentations, or rock bands to keep our kids in church. Expect love to solve these problems. Love never fails! (1 Corinthians 13:8).

Now go and do it! Transform your church into the caring community young people need. Take the first big step—learn their names.

Adolescents and Sexually Transmitted Disease

It not uncommon to hear that abstinence for sexual behavior before marriage is just a religious philosophy and that young people should be allowed or even encouraged to explore their sexuality before marriage. But, in fact, there are excellent reasons why young people are not developmentally ready for sex.

Dr. Allan Handysides, Director of Health Ministries for the General Conference of the Seventh-day Adventist Church is uniquely qualified to discuss this issue. Dr. Handysides is a physician who is board certified in both pediatrics and obstetrics-gynecology. He addressed this issue with the following comments:

Working as a gynecologist gives a person access to the private lives of many people. In this type of relationship, trust and confidentiality are major concerns. Physicians must often be silent about their own values as they treat their patients for fear that a patient will feel guilty or angry and refuse to share important behaviors or symptoms. Now that I am retired from clinical practice, I feel that I can freely share my experience and values without inhibiting some needy patient from expressing her cares or concerns to me.

I remember Mrs. K, sitting, weeping in my office after a trip to Ottawa, where she had accompanied her boss to help with the business deal. "I feel so dirty, so disloyal—a cheat," she cried. She had succumbed to the influence of a few drinks, seduction and pressure, and spent the night in bed with her boss. She was married, had two children, and a husband she loved. But, for lack of wisdom and a clearly focused set of values, and because she had normal hormone functions, she had flunked the test.

Another young woman—beautiful and well educated—asked, "Doctor, what do you think it is?"

I was looking at some red-edged little blisters, a few of which had burst, clustered on the edge of her genitals. "Well, I can't be a 100 percent certain. I need to test it."

"But what do you think?"

I could only answer, "Well, I will test it for herpes simplex."

She began to sob. "That never goes away, does it?"

She was right. I tried to be comforting. "Well, it dies down for long periods . . . "

"But I'm not even married," she cried.

I could just see the ad in the personal columns: *Herpes-positive female seeks herpes-male.* I said, "If you are really in love with this guy, you can marry and bear the problem together."

"But I don't want to marry him. He's really not my type," she answered.

I didn't say anything, but couldn't help wondering why she would sleep with someone not her "type." The power of a "rub and a tickle"— oh no! It's much more than that; and we must not forget it.

One day, a husband came. "I'm feeling dreadful," he said. I knew his beautiful wife was also extremely depressive and pessimistic. "You know how it is with my wife," he said. "I couldn't take it much longer and went out and picked this girl up. Now I'm worried sick I may have a disease or something. I know you're a gynecologist, but I know you best of all the doctors. Could you test me?"

Sad lives. Sometimes, sordid lives. The young pregnant girl asked, "Can you tell me who the father is?"

"How do you mean?" I asked.

She explained, "Well, see, I figure I must have gotten pregnant the week of the sixth to the thirteenth. On the Wednesday, I had sex with a guy I met at the bar. Then Friday and the weekend I was with my boyfriend, and the next Tuesday I met this other fellow . . ."

Each one of these stories is a true case, neither embellished nor altered, except for not giving names. I found myself in conversations like these every few days. If adults have problems like these with sexuality, what about adolescents?

Most people do not have a clear set of values when it comes to sexuality. So many people think of sex as no more than a little affectionate interlude, without *implications, complications,* or *commitment.* And that is precisely where the trouble lies.

Human sexuality *has implications.* Regardless of all the arguments, it is one of the most important ingredients in the glue that binds couples together. Compatibility, intellectual equality, friendship, and emotional balance are important, but sexuality has always been a critical part of the bonding. If it is becomes a common thing, shared with any and all, or even with a series of partners in "serial monogamy," much of its potency, mystique and power is dissipated. This is one of the most important implications of "free love"—it weakens the bonds of marriage.

There are also *complications* to unrestrained expression of sexuality in today's world. These are seen in the sexually transmitted diseases.

Adults have become uncertain of their own values when it comes to sex. The loud voices of those who recommend unlimited sexuality have cowed the majority—even those who sense that there is value in fidelity, trust, loyalty and the marriage vows.

If we are to teach our children values, we have to believe values, practice values, and teach values. It is impossible to pass such intimate nuances along without clear and strong relationships between parents and children, and parent and parent.

Many studies confirm that connectedness—a bonding in loving relationships—is the single most important factor in reducing at-risk behaviors such as sexual promiscuity in our youth.

The National Study on Adolescents shows that parents whose views are made clear to their children—both in the way they live and in what they say—have an effect on the behavior of their children, even though the views may be disputed and argued over. Parents need to talk straight and to know their facts. Young people need to know the facts too.

SO WHAT ARE THE FACTS?

Because of changes in the behavior of young people, there has been a significant increase in health-related problems in the area of sexuality. But this change demonstrates that *restrained behavior* is a realistic possibility because obviously behavior had been restrained before. Adolescents need to learn about sexuality and sexually transmitted diseases and be given guidance in an effort to change behavior and prevent infection and its spread.

Sexually transmitted diseases are a major cause of infertility, ectopic pregnancy, disease transmission to the newborn, malignancy, chronic illness, and even death (*Obstetric Clinics of North America,* Vol. 27, No. 1, March 2000, page 163).

Each year, about three million adolescents acquire a sexually transmitted disease in the U.S.A. This means about one in four sexually experienced teens acquire an infection. These odds are very high (Alan Guttmacher Institute: *Sex and America's Teenagers,* New York, 1997, page 38).

Chlamydial infections are a cause of considerable concern, rising to almost epidemic levels among girls less than 18 years of age. It is three times more common in this age group than in older women (CDC, *MMWR Morbidity/Mortality Weekly Report* 44 [RR-2], 1-102, 1995). In some groups, the rate may be as high as 29 percent of sexually active teenage women (Alan Guttmacher Institute: *Sex and America's Teenagers,* New York, 1997, page 38).

Younger adolescent girls are hospitalized more for pelvic inflammatory disease—tubal infections that can damage fertility—than older women. Several studies have demonstrated up to 50 percent of sexually experienced girls are infected with the Human Papilloma Virus (HPV). Health care costs associated with the treatment of STDs and their effects have been estimated at $5 billion (Washington and Katz, *JAMA,* 226:2565, 1991).

Many factors contribute to the high rates of STDs in adolescents. The social climate of secular thinking encourages sexual permissiveness. Risky behavior in exploring sexual activity is often magnified by the adolescent's relative lack of foresight and comprehension of consequences. Youthful attitudes of fatalism and invincibility make many youth "daredevils." They believe "it won't happen to me," or "if I'm meant to get it, so what can I do?"

Early sexual intercourse is often a symptom of other troubles, as shown by its association with sexual abuse, substance abuse, legal trouble, and mixing with an older set of companions (*J. Adolescent Health,* 17:83–90, 1995). And as adolescents age, they are more likely to engage in sexual activity. At 15 years of age, 20 to 40 percent of girls have had sexual intercourse. By age 17, this increases to 60 to 70 percent (CDC, *MMWR Weekly Report,* 45]55-4):64, 1996).

Adolescents are less likely to use barrier methods of contraception and protection—only 31 percent report regular use—and are more likely to have multiple partners (*J. School Health* 61:160–165, 1991; *Pediatrics* 85:24–29, 1990).

In young adolescence, the female cervix is covered with thin columnar epithelium, which is called ectropion. This condition makes the adolescent more vulnerable to sexually transmitted micro-organisms; local immunity is not as well-developed, and active cellular change—called metaplasia—helps the cervix be a reservoir for infection. Many adolescents also experience back-flow of menstrual blood through their tubes, which may spread sexually transmitted disease up into the reproductive tract. And a lack of insurance and concerns about confidentiality keep many adolescents from seeking timely and appropriate care (*JAMA* 269: 1404–1407; 1993; *JAMA* 273:1913–1918; 1995; *J Adolescent Health* 22:271–277; 1998).

In 1996, the American Medical Association issued Guidelines for Adolescent Preventive Services (GAPS) (AMA Monograph 1996, pp. 1–40). Among these guidelines is a recommendation that all sexually active adolescents receive health guidance annually, "regarding responsible sexual behaviors, including abstinence, latex condoms to prevent STDs including HIV infection."

This monograph recommends annual screening for STDs, including gonorrhea, chlamydia and if more than one sexual partner, syphilis and HIV. These recommendations underscore the anxiety with which the medical community views the seriousness of the dangers to which young people are exposing themselves by sexual promiscuity.

Types of Sexually Transmitted Diseases:
Genital Ulcers (affect both sexes):

The two classic ulcer-causing infections are (1) Herpes simplex virus infections, and (2) Syphilitic infection. Type I or Type II herpes simplex lesions may be smaller ulcers and more painful than the syphilitic chancre, though 3 to 11 percent of times, both infections may be present together (CDC MMWR Morbidity/Mortality Weekly Report 42 [RR-14]: 23, 1993).

Ulcers increase considerably the risk of acquiring HIV infection. Specific tests are required for diagnosis, and contacts should be tested if syphilis is diagnosed.

Genital warts (affect both sexes):

Human Papiloma Virus (HPV) infection is increasingly common. Over a three-year period, sexually active female college students had a cumulative incidence of 43 percent (*NEJM* 338:423–428, 1998). Most HPV infections show no symptoms and are not recognized. There are over twenty subtypes that can involve the genital tract. External warts are usually caused by subtypes 6 or 11, whereas subtypes 16 and 18 are more often a cause of cervical dysplasias. Sometimes, the warts can become large and treatments are less than satisfactory at times. In females, the need for Pap smear follow-up must be stressed, as HPV infection is felt to be a leading cause of cervical cancer.

Females may suffer from:
Vaginitis:

Inflammation of the vagina, when caused by a sexually transmitted disease (and more are not) is usually caused by trichomonas, or bacterial vaginosis. Trichomonas vaginalis has been isolated from 8 to 16 percent of sexually active adolescent women having vaginal examinations (*Pediatric Dermatology* 6:275–288, 1989).

Cervicitis:

Chlamydial infection is the most common cause infecting up to 29 percent of sexually active teenage women. As there are commonly no symptoms with this infection, all sexually active teens should be routinely screened, every six months (*JAMA* 280:521–526, 1998).

An estimated 600,000 new infections of gonorrhea occur annually. Though most show symptoms, a few are hidden unless pelvic inflammation reveals the infection. Newer tests are making the diagnosis easier and more reliable.

Pelvic Inflammatory Disease:
This is when an infection spreads through the internal female reproductive tract, involving the cervix, the uterus, the tubes, and ovaries, and causes peritonitis. Constant lower abdominal pain in a sexually active adolescent should raise suspicion of Pelvic Inflammatory Disease. Screening tests are mandatory.

Hepatitis B (affects both sexes):
This is the only sexually transmissible disease preventable through vaccination. It is highly contagious, and is a real threat in un-immunized adolescents. Approximately 250,000 new cases each year occur in the USA, of which 30 to 60 percent are sexually acquired (CDC *MMWR* 47[RR-1] 81–118, 1998).

Human Immunodeficiency Virus (affects both sexes):
Youths 13 to 22 years of age account for nearly 25 percent of the new cases reported in the USA (CDC Fact Sheet, March 1998, pp. 1–2). Transmission patterns are becoming more heterosexual, though drug usage and sharing of needles account for over 25 percent of new cases.

This overview shows the need for guidance among today's youth. Such guidance can only be given where relationships of trust and freedom from criticism exist. Parents, mentors, and peers all own the burden of prevention and care, for we are indeed our younger brothers' and sisters' keepers.